Fighting in the Sky

Acknowledgements

The painters whose work is at the core of this book are credited in the text and have been a principal inspiration to the author. The Royal Air Force museums at Hendon, Duxford and Elvington and the Imperial War Museum in London, as well as the museums under the auspices of the Smithsonian in Washington, have been great and most helpful sources for the pictures.

Sian Phillips of the Bridgeman Art library has been a most knowledgeable adviser, and George Chamier the most careful and creative editor.

Fighting in the Sky

The Story in Art

John Fairley

Pen & Sword
MILITARY

First published in Great Britain in 2020 by
Pen & Sword Aviation
An imprint of
Pen & Sword Books Ltd
Yorkshire – Philadelphia

ISBN 978 1 52676 220 7

Typeset by Mac Style
Printed and bound by Printworks Global Ltd, London/Hong Kong.

Pen & Sword Books Limited incorporates the imprints of Atlas, Archaeology, Aviation, Discovery, Family History, Fiction, History, Maritime, Military, Military Classics, Politics, Select, Transport, True Crime, Air World, Frontline Publishing, Leo Cooper, Remember When, Seaforth Publishing, The Praetorian Press, Wharncliffe Local History, Wharncliffe Transport, Wharncliffe True Crime and White Owl.

For a complete list of Pen & Sword titles please contact

PEN & SWORD BOOKS LIMITED
47 Church Street, Barnsley, South Yorkshire, S70 2AS, England
E-mail: enquiries@pen-and-sword.co.uk
Website: www.pen-and-sword.co.uk

Or

PEN AND SWORD BOOKS
1950 Lawrence Rd, Havertown, PA 19083, USA
E-mail: Uspen-and-sword@casematepublishers.com
Website: www.penandswordbooks.com

Contents

Acknowledgements   ii
Picture Credits   vii
Preface   ix
Introduction   xi

Part I   The First World War   1

Part II   The Second World War   53

Part III Post-1945   119

Epilogue   138
Appendix   139

Picture Credits

Page viii – Eagle Squadron memorial, 1985 (bronze) Frink, Elisabeth (1930–93). (*Photo © www.LondonRemembers.com*)

Page xi – Stealth, 1995 (foil and acrylic on canvas) Kalkhof, Peter (b.1933). (© *IWM* (*Art.IWM ART 16824*)/© *Peter Kalkhof/Annely Juda Fine Art*)

Page 5 – Bombardement De Dieuze Par Une Escadrille D'avions Voisin, 1917 (oil on canvas) Farré, Henri (1871–1934). (© *Photo: National Air and Space Museum Collection/Gift of Mr Fay Leone Faurote/Smithsonian*)

Page 6 – The French aviator Georges Guynemer, 1917 (watercolour on paper) Farré, Henri (1871–1934). (*Bridgeman Images*)

Page 7 – 45e Victoire Du Capitaine Guynemer, 1917 (oil on canvas) Farré, Henri (1871–1934). (© *Photo: National Air and Space Museum Collection/Gift of Mr Fay Leone Faurote/Smithsonian*)

Page 9 – A Soldier's Death 1915, Farré, Henri (1871–1934). (*Image courtesy of Hindman Auctions*)

Page 10 – Dogfight, 1916 (oil on canvas), Farré, Henri (1871–1934). (© *Photo: Heritage Auctions, HA.com*)

Page 11 – Portrait of Heurteaux, 1917 (oil on canvas), Farré, Henri (1871–1934). (© *Photo: National Air and Space Museum Collection/Gift of Mr Fay Leone Faurote/Smithsonian*)

Page 16 – One down, four to go (self-portrait), 1960 (oil on canvas), Fowler, Mel (1921–87) (*Photo: Alexander Historical Auctions/Estate of Mel Fowler*)

Page 18 – The first Zeppelin seen from Piccadilly Circus, 8 September 1915 (oil on canvas), Gow, Andrew Carrick (1848–1920). (*IWM, London, UK/Bridgeman Images*)

Page 20 – A Convoy, North Sea, 1918. From NS 7: painted from an airship off the coast of Norway, 1918 (oil on canvas), Lavery, John (1856–1941). (© *IWM* (*Art.IWM ART 1257*))

Page 22 – An Aerial Fight, 1918 (oil on canvas), Weirter, Louis (1893–1932). (*IWM, London, UK/Bridgeman Images*)

Page 24 – Honorary Air Marshal William Avery Bishop (oil on canvas), Jongers, Alphonse (1872–1945). (*CWM 19680068.001/Beaverbrook Collection of War Art/Canadian War Museum*)

Page 26 – The Last Flight of Captain Ball VC, DSO and 2 Bars, MC, 7 May 1917, painted 1919 (watercolour on paper), Arnold, Norman G. (1892–1963). (*IWM, London, UK/Bridgeman Images*)

Page 30 – Parachuting: the Destruction of a Kite Balloon by a German Aeroplane, Doiran Front, 1917 (watercolour on paper), Wood, William T. (1877–1958). (© *IWM* (*Art.IWM ART 795*))

Page 31 – A Parachute-landing (oil on panel), Pitchforth, Roland Vivian (1895–1982). (© *IWM* (*Art.IWM ART LD 3189*))

Page 32 – Attack on a Balloon and Dogfight (lithographs), Bridgman, Leonard (1895–1980).

Page 35 – DH9 Biplane, Theobald, Tony.

Page 37 – British Scouts leaving their Aerodrome on Patrol, over the Asiago Plateau, Italy, 1918 (oil on canvas), Carline, Sydney (1888–1929). (*IWM, London, UK/Bridgeman Images*)

Page 38 – Sopwith Camel Patrol Attacking an Austrian Aerodrome near Sacile, Italy, 1918 (oil on board), Carline, Sydney (1888–1929). (*IWM, London, UK/Bridgeman Images*)

Page 39 – Machines and anti-aircraft fire above the Alps near the Valley of the Piave, 7 April 1918 (charcoal on paper), Carline, Sydney (1888–1929). (© *IWM* (*Art.IWM ART 4487*))

Page 41 – Baghdad, 1919 (oil on canvas) Carline, Richard (1896–1980). (© *IWM* (*Art.IWM ART 6348*))

Page 42 – Jerusalem and the Dead Sea from an aeroplane, 1919 (oil on canvas) Carline, Richard (1896–1980). (© *IWM* (*Art.IWM ART 3083*))

Page 43 – Siege of Kut-al-Amara seen from the air, 1919. British Maurice-Farman aeroplane approaching, attacked by enemy Fokker, 1919 (oil on canvas) Carline, Richard (1896–1980). (© *IWM* (*Art.IWM ART 6349*))

Page 45 – The city of Samarra and the desert with River Tigris, 1919 (oil on canvas), Carline, Richard (1896–1980). (© *IWM* (*Art.IWM ART 6351*))

Page 46 – Gaza seen from the air, over British lines on Ali Muntar Hill looking towards the sea, 1919 (oil on canvas), Carline, Richard (1896–1980). (© *IWM* (*Art.IWM ART 6350*))

Page 47 – Flying over the desert at sunset, Mesopotamia, 1919 (oil on canvas), Carline, Sydney (1888–1929). (© *IWM* (*Art.IWM ART 4623*))

Page 48 – Flying above Kirkuk, Kurdistan, 1919 (watercolour on paper), Carline, Sydney (1888–1929). (© *IWM* (*Art.IWM ART 4637*))

Page 49 – The destruction of the Turkish Transport in the Gorge of the Wadi Fara, Palestine, 1920 (oil on canvas), Carline, Sydney (1888–1929). (© *IWM* (*Art.IWM ART 3138*))

Page 51 – Guernica, 1937 (oil on canvas), Picasso, Pablo (1881–1973). (*Museo Nacional Centro de Arte Reina Sofia, Madrid, Spain/Bridgeman Images*)

Page 54 – Target area: Whitley bombers over Berlin, 1940 (watercolour and chalk on paper), Nash, Paul (1889–1946). (© *IWM* (*Art.IWM ART LD 827*))

Page 56 – Aircraft runway in course of construction at Thélus, near Arras, May 1940 (oil on canvas), Freedman, Barnett (1901–58). (*IWM, London, UK/Bridgeman Images*)

Page 57 – A CHL (Chain Home Low) radar station, 1945 (oil on canvas), Rawlinson, William Thomas (1912–93). (© *IWM (Art.IWM ART LD 5731)*)

Page 59 – Battle of Britain, 1941 (oil on canvas), Nash, Paul (1889–1946). (*IWM, London, UK/Bridgeman Images*)

Page 62 – Air-sea rescue from RAF Coltishall, Norfolk, 1981 (acrylic on canvas), Staden, Geoffrey (b.1953). (© *IWM (Art.IWM ART LD 4756)*)

Page 64 – Totes Meer (Dead Sea), 1940–41 (oil on canvas), Nash, Paul (1889–1946). (*Photo © Tate*)

Page 67 – (LD769) Air fight over Portland, 1940, Eurich, Richard Ernest (1903–92). (*IWM, London, UK/Bridgeman Images*)

Page 69 – Eagle Squadron Memorial, 1985 (bronze), Frink, Elisabeth (1930–93). (*Photo: www.LondonRemembers.com*)

Page 71 – The first Lancaster bomber to land in North Africa from England after bombing the German base at Friedrichshafen, which inaugurated a 'shuttle-bombing service', 1943 (w/c on paper), Stafford-Baker, Julius Barkis (1904–88). (*IWM, London, UK/Bridgeman Images/© The Estate of Julian Stafford-Baker*)

Page 73 – Battle of London: Royal Marine AA gunners bring down a flying bomb, 1944 (oil on canvas) Cole, Leslie (1910–77) / © IWM (Art.IWM ART LD 4514))

Page 74 – Battle of Germany, 1944 (oil on canvas), Nash, Paul (1889–1946). (*IWM, London, UK/Bridgeman Images*)

Page 76 – RAF club window (stained glass), Whittaker, Helen. (© *Helen Whittaker*)

Page 77 – Bomber Command Memorial, Hyde Park Corner. (*Adobe Stock*)

Page 79 – The destroyed Dresden, c.1952 (oil on canvas), Rudolph, Wilhelm (1889–1982). (*Staatliche Kunstsammlungen, Dresden, Germany/Bridgeman Images*)

Page 81 – HMS *Glorious* in the Arctic, 1940 (w/c on paper), Ravilious, Eric (1903–42). (*IWM, London, UK/Bridgeman Images*)

Page 84 – USAAF in Britain: Private First Class Barbara O'Brien paints the nose of a B-26 Marauder, Associated Press Photographer. (© *IWM (FRE 13539)*)

Page 85 – Flying Fortress (oil on canvas), Trudgian, Nicolas. (*Courtesy of Nicolas Trudgian, published by ValorStudios.com*)

Page 87 – Air gunner prepared for action (oil on paper), Cundall, Charles Ernest (1890–1971). (© *IWM (Art.IWM ART LD 6051)*)

Page 89 – Blue Baby, Blitz over Britain, 1941 (w/c on paper), Burra, Edward (1905–76). (*Private Collection/Photo © Lefevre Fine Art Ltd., London/Bridgeman Images*)

Page 90 – At night in the underground station between Mornington Crescent and Hampstead 1940 (ink on paper), Thornycroft, Priscilla (1917–2000). (© *IWM (Art. IWM ART 16508 8)*)

Page 91 – A Sunderland flying boat on patrol (oil on canvas), Burgess, Arthur (1879–1957). (© *IWM (Art.IWM ART LD 6003)*)

Page 95 – The Swordfish attack at Taranto (print), Taylor, Robert. (*Photo courtesy of Duke's Auctions*)

Page 96 – Attack on a convoy seen from the air, 1941 (oil on canvas), Eurich, Richard Ernst (1903–1992). (© *IWM (Art.IWM ART LD 1326)*)

Page 98 – Battle over Malta, 1942: Spitfire attacking Ju 88s in a dogfight with ME 109s, 1942 (oil on canvas), Barnham, Denis Alfred (1920–81). (© *IWM (Art.IWM ART LD 3960)*)

Page 101 – Crashed gliders: the landing-zone at Ranville, 1944 (w/c), Richards, Albert (1919–45). (*IWM, London, UK/Bridgeman Images*)

Page 102 – The Drop, 1944 (oil on panel), Richards, Albert (1919–45). (*IWM, London, UK/Bridgeman Images*)

Page 103 – A glider pilot at the controls, 1942 (oil on canvas), Cole, Leslie (1910–77). (© *IWM (Art.IWM ART LD 2644)*)

Page 105 – Rocket-firing Typhoons at the Falaise Gap, Normandy, 1944 (oil on canvas), Wootton, Frank (1911–98). (© *IWM (Art.IWM ART LD 4756)*)

Page 107 – A U-boat surrenders to a Hudson aircraft, 1941 (oil on canvas), Cundall, Charles Ernest (1890–1971). (© *IWM (Art.IWM ART LD 1561)*)

Page 108 – Sinking of the *Tirpitz* (lithograph), Wootton, Frank (1911–98). (© *Photo: Gunns Gallery/Estate of Frank Wootton*)

Page 110 – Verdun, 1917 (oil on canvas), Vallotton, Felix (1865–1925). (*Musée De l'Armée, Paris/Bridgeman Images*)

Page 112 – Kiirung, Formosa, 7 September 1945. The interior of a hidden Japanese hangar (watercolour and ink on paper), Morris, James (1908–89). (© *IWM (Art.IWM ART LD 5537)*)

Page 113 – 'Tora Tora Tora: The Attack' (oil on canvas), Shepherd, Stu. (© *Stu Shepherd*)

Page 114 – Airplane on carrier deck, Sourabaya, 1942 (gouache on paper), Plante, George (1914–95). (© *IWM (Art.IWM ART 17155)*)

Page 116 – A V2 rocket leaving Walcheren, 1944 (chalk on paper), Bone, Stephen (1904–58). (© *IWM (Art.IWM ART LD 4691)*)

Page 117 – Meteor Mk 1s in fly past over central London, 1945 (oil on canvas), Wootton, Frank (1911–1998). (*RAF Museum, on loan from the Society of British Aerospace Companies Limited*)

Page 120 – Airstrike, Taylor, Robert. (© *The Military Gallery*)

Page 123 – Vulcan, Tymon, Gary. (© *Gary Tymon*)

Page 128 – Falklands Diary: Argentine Pucaras, Kitson, Linda (b.1945). (*Art.IWM ART 15530 43*)

Page 129 – SS *Canberra*, San Carlos waters. Helicopters transferring supplies, 2–3 June 1982 (conte crayon on paper), Kitson, Linda (b.1945). (© *IWM (Art.IWM ART 15530 27)*)

Page 131 – Falklands Diary: helicopter on the deck of the *QE2,* Kitson, Linda (b.1945). (*Art.IWM ART 15530 3*)

Page 134 – 'Blue-Water Force', Wong, Ronald, FGAvA, 2019. (*Courtesy of the artist*)

Page 136 – Tornado, Woodcock, Keith. (© *Keith Woodcock*)

Page 140 – 'Sailor' Malan, Cuthbert, Orde (1888–1968).

Preface

When the sculptor Elisabeth Frink learned that her friend Linda Kitson was to go with the Task Force as the official war artist in the Falklands conflict, she wrote: 'Who could be a better choice? But at the same time I was alarmed that such a vulnerable person should be going at all.' Frink also reflected:

> I think that only an artist can portray in such a way the sadness and horror of war. There have been many brave photographers and cameramen whose fine pictures have shown us war in all its aspects. Artists give us another dimension, the little personal details of being in a battle as well as the big picture. Whether it is the stark landscape of a Sutherland or a Nash, or many others who, by their work, convey the different sides of war, the mind and eye of the artist is a very powerful lens.

Frink was to make a number of powerful memorials herself, including her goggled warriors and her great monument in London to the American Eagle Squadron pilots of the Second World War.

Poets, certainly, have wanted to express the exultancy of flight and the action in the skies. John Gillespie Magee, Spitfire pilot, left us what has become the great hymn to those moments of intensity.

Elisabeth Frink, Eagle Squadron memorial.

Oh, I have slipped the surly bonds of earth
And danced the skies on laughter-silvered wings.
Sunward I've climbed and joined the tumbling mirth
Of sun-split clouds – and done a hundred things
You have not dreamed of – wheeled and soared and swung
High in the sunlit silence. Hovering there
I've chased the shouting wind along and flung
My eager craft through footless halls of air.
Up, up, the long delirious burning blue,
I've topped the windswept heights with easy grace
Where never lark, or ever eagle flew.
And while, with silent lifting mind, I've trod
The high untrespassed sanctity of space,
Put out my hand, and touched the face of God.

But it fell to the artists and airmen from the first days of war in the air – barely a decade after Orville Wright's first powered flight – to look to capture, in their pictures, the almost unimaginable experience of fighting in the skies.

The era of man-to-man combat in the heavens was to last barely a century. It is now almost over. But in that time the artists gave us a vision at which the world has marvelled and wondered.

Introduction

Peter Kalkhof's imagining of a Stealth bomber, transparent, translucent and otherworldly, is set over the landscape which has seen most of its active use in combat – the desert. In less than a century, fighting in the sky has moved from pilots shooting pistols at each other above the trenches to this ghostly predator from the furthest atmosphere.

The American forces have used Stealth aircraft, over Syria in 2018, over Libya and, most remarkably, in the first Gulf War in Iraq. Though they constituted less than three per cent of the US Air Force contingent, they accounted for more than 40 per cent of the strategic targets which were taken out. The Nighthawk, the Spirit, the Raptor and the Lightning 11 are all American stealth planes.

Stealth technology, aimed at making planes virtually undetectable to hostile aircraft or radar, or simply to human vision, has a long history. Even in the First World War, the Germans experimented by covering planes with see-through cellulose, though none saw service before the war ended. And then in the Second World War the Germans tried building planes with plywood.

By the 1970s, Lockheed's designers in America were working on a fuselage made of angled panels which directed radar away from its return path. They were also trying to diminish infrared output in order to deceive heat-seeking missiles.

The Spirit was used in the Kosovo campaign in Yugoslavia in 1999, flying nonstop all the way from its base in Missouri and back again. The Kosovo War of 1999 was, arguably, the first and only war won solely by air power; it was the first time German Air Force planes had been in combat since the Second World War; and it saw the first loss of a stealth fighter in combat, when a missile brought down an American Air Force Nighthawk. This loss, when the plane came down relatively intact in Serbian territory, offered the first chance for Serbia's Russian allies to examine how Stealth planes were constructed – the whole Stealth project having been developed by Lockheed in conditions of the greatest, and successfully guarded, secrecy.

Then a Stealth helicopter actually crashed in the grounds of Osama bin Ładen's villa in 2011 during the operation to capture and kill him.

The Stealth planes have developed from the extraordinary line of aircraft built to help mankind's new warriors of the third dimension conquer their enemies in the heavens. The first experience of war in the air, in the Great War, was literally unimaginable, except to the pilots themselves.

Peter Kalkhof, Stealth.

Photography could do little to express the extraordinary manoeuvres, the terrors and the excitements of these encounters. But a number of the early pilots were also distinguished artists, and their paintings provoked astonished admiration when they were first shown in a London gallery. But through the post-war Imperial campaigns in the Middle East, the exploits of the Spitfires in the Battle of Britain, and on to the most recent conflicts, as in Iraq, where British planes were still being shot down, the artists' evocation of the drama and thrills of fighting in the sky have been the most effective and emotional representation of the fliers' role.

Alongside these paintings, the most vivid written accounts also came from the pilots themselves – even in those very early years, some of them were expressing it all in poetry.

These first paintings from the skies were to have an acute and lasting influence on art. When the *Horizon* critic first saw Sydney Carline's paintings in a post-war exhibition in London he tried to convey the excitement of seeing 'this new and strange point of view'.

This all came at a time of turmoil and adventure in Western art. Cubism had thrust its angular theory into the Paris art world. Malevich was preaching Suprematism. Indeed, he was one of the first to use the perspectives of the sky in his painting. It is possible to discern the red shapes of aeroplanes and the unseen horizons in his work. Meanwhile, the Futurists were preaching idolatry of the machine.

Part I

The First World War

The First Military Plane

When Orville and Wilbur Wright sold the first ever military aeroplane to the US Army in 1909, its clearly stated purpose was to be as a means of reconnaissance. Half a century earlier, both sides in the American Civil War had found that manned balloons could give a better view of opposing forces and their disposition than anyone at ground level. But the new powered aircraft offered the possibility of seeing much more than was possible from a tethered balloon. The Wright Military Flyer covered more than 40 miles in its acceptance trials.

It was not only in America that military men quickly grasped the advantages of flight. Within a decade, the Italians were using planes to scout out what their Turkish enemies were doing in the war they were fighting in North Africa. And the French, inspired by Louis Blériot, were developing a range of aircraft, including the Voisin, the Caudron and the Breguet.

Among the crowds of Americans enjoying the Paris of the pre-war era was a self-described soldier of fortune called Bert Hall from Bowling Green, Kentucky. In 1910 he took himself down to the field at Buc, south of Versailles, where Maurice Farman was based. He said: 'The first plane I ever had under

my own control was a Maurice Farman Biplane Pusher with a fog cutter out in front and an air-cooled Renault motor behind.' There was room for two in the cockpit. 'They were just about as manoeuvrable as a cow – *vaches méchaniques*, we called them.'

At first the machine just lifted a few feet off the ground and then landed again. 'I taxied that mechanical cow over the little field a good long while and watched Maurice Farman a lot before I finally opened up the throttle for a take-off. I really took off about two or three feet. Then I cut the motor and made a landing. It was thrilling indeed to be free of the earth.'

Hall soon found himself a delighted aviator and in 1911 bought one of Blériot's new planes. Then word reached him that the Sultan of Turkey, Abdul Hamid, was looking to establish an Air Force in his war with Bulgaria. Promised a fee supposed to be $100 a day, Hall lost no time in taking his Blériot on a long series of hops across Central Europe to the area round Adrianople, where the war – largely a matter of old fashioned cavalry charges and infantry attacks – had become a stalemate. The Sultan's gold was duly proffered, and Hall embarked on one of the earliest ventures in war flying.

As Hall recounted in his memoirs, which were accompanied by a series of dramatic paintings and drawings by his friend Leonard Bridgman, 'It was largely a question of looking at the state of the opposing Bulgarian forces.' But they were keen enough to shoot at him – although, as he said, they must have been terrible shots because there were no holes to be found in his plane when he landed.

But, in true soldier of fortune style, when Hall discovered his gold was not being paid in the agreed quantities, he simply took off and, via Romania, offered his services to the Bulgarians. He found the Turks couldn't hit his plane either. But once again the remuneration came up short, and Hall found himself locked up and threatened with the firing squad. He only got out when his French observer contrived to bribe the right Bulgarians to get him and the plane back to Romania, and then on a long circuit to France, via numerous sufficiently lucrative air demonstrations, just in time for the outbreak of war in 1914.

He rapidly talked himself into the new French air service – this time actually armed with a rifle and metal darts, which were the first offensive weapons of the air war. The darts – steel-tipped *flèchettes*, as they were called – were simply thrown from the plane once it was over the German trenches.

Hall was to survive the Great War flying an array of French aircraft, with rapidly improving weaponry.

The Russian

The new excitement of flight and then the prospect, and soon the reality, of war, gave an enormous impetus in many countries to the development of the aeroplane.

The Tsar Nicholas II had already, by 1912, established a school of aviation in St Petersburg, and it was from there that a young man called Pyotr Nestorov first brought off the outrageous manoeuvre of looping the loop. This was done in a Nieuport monoplane over an airfield at Syertsk, near Kiev. For his pains, he was disciplined for hazarding his new aircraft.

Undaunted, he entered the Russian Air Force in 1914, only to try another improbable tactic of flying his Morane Saulnier straight at an Austrian reconnaissance aircraft. Neither, in those early days of the war, was armed, although Nestorov perhaps thought he could damage his opponent and survive. But both planes crashed, and both pilots died.

After the first brief period of the Great War, when flyers, armed only with pistols and rifles, rarely attacked enemy planes, young airmen soon discovered how quickly they could turn, how they could spin and spiral downwards and still come out of a dive, and how they could roll their craft.

The First Frenchman

The French artist Henri Farré was the true pioneer of painting the fighting in the sky. From the first months of the Great War he was depicting his own personal experiences to produce superb paintings of all aspects of the new world of combat in the air.

Farré, already forty years old, was living in Argentina, at the Plaza hotel in Buenos Aires, when news of the outbreak of the war arrived. He recalled:

I saw a long and solid mass coming down Florida Street. An intense heat hung over the city. The shouts of the crowd reached my ears, muffled and mellowed through the heavy atmosphere. I ran downstairs to the lobby where a polyglot mob was assembled, some with shame written on their faces. Germans were talking amongst themselves in low voices, evidently suppressing an ill-concealed joy. They were mostly business men or brokers happy to see the great day arrive.

Farré immediately decided to return to France, but he had to wait two weeks before he could find a place on a ship bound for Europe. There were already German cruisers off the Argentine coast. The delay allowed him to witness the massed crowds in the Argentine capital, where 'The people, almost to a man, shuddered with undisguised horror and hate of the Germans.'

Farré's trip home aboard the *Lutetia* with a couple of thousand Army reservists was something of a cat-and-mouse journey, avoiding enemy shipping.

As soon as he arrived in Bordeaux he went straight to Paris, where he contrived to meet General Nioux, who ran the French Army Museum. Nioux had already been authorized to appoint some official painters to, as he said, 'immortalize on canvas true pictures of fighting in the field'.

'Would you like to be a painter of aviation?' Nioux enquired.

Within days, Farré found himself attached to a squadron of Voisin bombers, under Lieutenant Mouchard. It was still only December 1914, and Farré learned from Mouchard that the old code of martial courtesies still held good. Seeing German planes nearby in the air, the Lieutenant said that it never occurred to airmen to fire at each other. In any case, the pilots only carried revolvers. Indeed, Farré was present when a package arrived wrapped in a French flag which had been dropped by a German aircraft. Inside was a letter from a French pilot who had been forced to land behind German lines. The letter read: 'I must testify to the German officers' gallant attitude towards us, and I wish to thank them now for having afforded us a means to communicate with you.'

There was then a note requesting information about two German flyers who had come down behind French lines, and the French duly returned the favour with an information package dropped to the Germans.

Farré was determined to get himself into the air as soon as possible. A Lieutenant de Clerck agreed to take him up on a reconnaissance flight:

At first I did not feel that we were flying. But as we climbed, the panorama expanded and the horizon followed. All at once I noticed a burst of black smoke appear, and then three or four more about three hundred yards away. 'What's that?' I enquired of de Clerck. 'Those are Boche cannon shots', he replied. 'I don't consider that very alarming,' I said. 'Just wait,' he said. As we crossed the enemy lines, the Boche artillery saluted our passage. One shell burst quite close.

On the way home, through clouds and continuing fire, Farré saw that the pilot was writing and simply using his knees to steer the tiller of the plane. It turned out to be a letter to the pilot's wife. But from that moment, on that first flight, Farré realized that he could sketch and draw the action around him while flying. These drawings were to be the basis of the great body of work which he was to produce.

In short order, Farré found himself flying with a bomb release lever in one hand and a drawing pad in the other. A pilot, Lieutenant Fernand, volunteered to take him on a bombing run over a German Army transport centre, 40km behind the front line. Farré recorded:

It was a beautiful night. At first my eyes were blinded by the passing rays of searchlights. I could see absolutely nothing. Little by little I recovered my normal vision. There was a village just beneath us, the houses apparently in ruins. I could make out the roads and a little river reflecting the silvery light of the moon.

Even then he was sketching. There were rockets and fires, he wrote, detonating with all the colours of the rainbow, and 'Further back, I saw an immense light. It was the city of Verdun burning. High in the heavens and not far above us, great shells were bursting.'

But soon they neared their target, and Farré had to earn his flight ticket. It was his job to release the bombs, and he saw seven explosions as the bombs dropped. But they were armed with eight bombs. 'I pushed my arm into the bomb release', he recalled, 'and then looked outside, when, horror of horrors, there it was, suspended from a cable underneath our machine.'

Pilot Fernand said they had to get rid of it; they would be blown to pieces if they tried to land like that. Farré tried to cut the steel cable with his knife, to no avail. Finally he managed to haul the bomb back up – 'It was 15 kilos. I managed to raise it above my head and then threw it down with all my strength.'

The cable parted and the bomb dropped: 'I looked down and saw the bomb had exploded in a beautiful and innocent piece of work.'

They got safely back, and this bombing misadventure did not deter Farré from constant further flying. He was soon in observation planes and this time, his side job, apart from being an official artist, was to man the machine gun. On an early flight they were hardly over the German lines when a large biplane appeared.

'That's a Rumpler', said the Captain. 'Hit him.'

They steered straight for him, but he passed about 200 metres to the right. Farré opened up with his machine gun, to no effect:

But what should suddenly I see high in the air above us like a meteor, our comrade Navarre in his red plane, a veritable bird of prey swooping down on the poor Rumpler. A volley from his machine gun set fire to its gasoline tank. Quick as lightning the plane fell, trailing behind an enormous tail of smoke. The conqueror swept in a spiral of glory around that colossal torch as it descended from the heavens, an easy victory for him.

Henri Farré, Bombardment of Dieuze.

Henri Farré, Commandant Guynemer.

Henri Farré, *Victory of Commandant Guynemer.*

Farré landed to find Navarre stretched out relaxing under the wing of his plane, and happy to concede that he had quite blatantly used Farré's plane as bait.

But Farré's greatest hero among all the French – and indeed, American – aviators with whom he lived was Commandant Guynemer. He made a series of paintings of the Commandant's exploits, including the time he so confounded a German pilot as to persuade him to land on Guynemer's home airfield, apparently greatly relieved that he had been captured by France's most renowned air ace.

Farré painted Guynemer's victories, until his final flight, which his Lieutenant, Bozon Verduras, described to Farré:

All at once several hostile planes rose out of the clouds. I myself attacked the new arrivals and succeeded in dispersing them. I then turned around and looked for my dear comrade. Alas, in all the immensity of that sea of clouds, I could see no trace of Guynemer. His plane had disappeared.

Farré went on flying and painting and was to survive the war with perhaps the greatest collection of first-hand-experience works of art of all the painters of the war in the air.

Diligently pursuing the reality and, indeed, the fear and excitement of fighting in the air, Farré also made a point of collecting written accounts of their experiences from some of his comrades. This is a 1917 letter from Commandant Heurtaux:

Dear Chief,

I am very much behind in writing to you, and I hope you will excuse my long silence. I have just gone through a very trying time and have suffered much with my wounds, owing to supervening complications. Now I am finally able to pull through and somewhat re-established in health, and I am attempting to make up for lost time.

You have asked me for a story of a fight in the air, and I am going to narrate one of my latest experiences, although it is not of a very recent date. You know that I had no sooner returned to the front than I was again wounded.

We had just arrived in a new locality. The first days were passed in arranging our hangars, and particularly in very carefully overhauling our machines, which had considerably run down during our long period of activity.

On several occasions already, the Boches had been flying over our heads, taking advantage of our forced inaction. From the ground we could distinguish their black crosses, not without cursing our inability to pursue them. Finally, the machines were ready; it was beautiful weather – not a cloud in the sky. A strong wind was blowing but it was at least favourable for an excursion against the enemy. I had great hopes, therefore, of being able to give him battle and to return without being too much knocked up.

Everything was carefully straightened out on board. I got in and was trying the motor when suddenly some white tufts appeared over our heads, and in their midst – a

Henri Farré, A Soldier's Death.

plane; no doubt about it; it was an enemy arriving just at the proper time.

I let go in all haste, without losing sight of the bursting shells which gave me my proper course. I went up as rapidly as possible; the motor worked beautifully, so I could soon make out my enemy. It was without question a reconnoitring plane, flying around over its objective, taking photographs. So much the better! In that case the observer would be less likely to notice my presence.

I tried out the machine gun and tested all my instruments for the last time, as I had arrived in the danger zone. Everything was going well, and all I had to do was to begin the fight.

The Boche was about eight hundred metres off – seven hundred metres yet to run before opening fire. I approached him rapidly; a few little white clouds appeared in front of me; I was discovered. The gunner had already commenced firing; it looked as if the fight would be a hot one, and I began zigzagging at once, so as to destroy his aim. The little white tufts were growing farther and farther away; all was well. Our distance apart diminished more and more.

The machine-gun volleys now lasted longer, a good sign that the enemy was getting excited. We still drew together, and I could make out clearly the shapes of the pilot and passenger; but I saw I must get closer. Finally I could see the face of the machine-gunner very clearly. I was at good range, and it was now my turn to reply. At the first shot the Boche commenced to fire, then to dive more and more.

The two machine guns rattled away without pause, and the enemy tried in vain to escape, until after some sharp turns his machine suddenly began to descend – the pilot must have been shot – and this manoeuvre of his brought me very suddenly into his arc of fire. A few shots – sudden noises around me – a violent blow in the left leg – am I wounded? I shake myself, but can't discover anything; I am flooded with water, with gasoline; a sudden moment of fear – shall I take fire? No smoke, thank God!

Henri Farré, Dogfight.

Henri Farré, Commandant Heurtaux.

And now what had become of my adversary? These few seconds had given him time to take a fresh position. My motor stopped; how should I be able to continue the fight? Luck followed me, however; the Boche at once began to turn his nose down. I flew in his wake, joined him, and so took up a most beautiful commanding position.

Again I commenced firing at him, never letting him go. We fell vertically, going like mad. The machine gun crackled incessantly, but the enemy never replied. Finally my ammunition gave out; I had to abandon my prize.

It was now high time to think of myself and to select a landing-place, not an easy thing to find in this hilly region. I finally discovered a little strip of land close to a wood; it was the only possible place. The high wind allowed me to come to earth slowly in the midst of holes and logs, which I finally did without accident. I jumped out of my machine in haste, and found it in a very sad condition, indeed, completely unfit for service. As for me, some shots had gone through my teddy bear. I was fully repaid by my adventure.

A little while later, an automobile picked me up and took me back to camp. There I found – with much pleasure – that my German had fallen within our lines, and was still burning on the ground. I went to look at the wreck, and that same night started out to look for a new machine which would allow me to begin again.

Goodbye, my dear Chief. I hope that luck will favour us and that we may soon see each other again. I send you a cordial handshake.

Heurtaux

Reconnaissance and the Strategists

Reconnaissance was the chief task of the first planes to reach the battlefields of the Great War, as the armies developed the almost impenetrable barriers of the trench system. But it was the pilots themselves who were the first to appreciate that their planes offered them the possibility of a much more active role than as mere observers.

The most obvious tactic was to drop explosives on the men and weapons they could see below them. The French Army was the first to start developing planes specifically for that role – and the Voisin bombers duly appeared.

In a remarkable letter, one of the early Voisin pilots, Lieutenant Partridge, described to Henri Farré, in almost lyrical fashion, the nature and satisfactions of this new phenomenon of delivering war from the air. Indeed, the Lieutenant sets out in detail the strategy and purpose of aerial bombing which was to hold good right through to the Second World War and beyond. Although, perhaps, few bomber pilots subsequently felt entitled to express such joy in their occupation as Partridge took in the pleasure of distributing mayhem on to the troops and landscape below him:

Dear Chief,

What is my opinion in regard to bombarding? I can explain it by saying only that, from the very first trial of this method, I have devoted myself to it entirely; and as the attraction is so strong I shall be only too glad to give you my ideas concerning it and the principles which have convinced me of its value.

From the very beginning, bombarding by aeroplanes offered to me a strong attraction by reason of its apparently unlimited destructive power. After the early experimental period was over, you will remember our great raids of 1915, which confirmed a success made possible by tentative effort in this direction. This side of aviation is most captivating, the source of impressions which it is impossible to feel in any other branch of the service.

The great beauty of a departure at sunrise; the evolutions of the little flotilla; then the crossing of the lines and the heading to the east; no more trenches, no more impassable wall; one flies to the enemy, seeking him at rest.

Lorraine – the Vosges – Alsace – the Rhine, and then – Germany. The factories first feel the destructive force of the planes; then the cities beyond the Rhine – in order to avenge the German lust and the innocent victims of our unfortified cities – then no weak hesitation.

The danger may increase – but what is the difference! With that feeling of absolute detachment from terrestrial things; the spirit free, and without care of bullet or gun, they steer straight to the end in view, drinking in all the beauties of the voyage, and enjoying the ideal sensations to which it gives birth, in anticipation of a perfect accomplishment of the mission in hand.

That is the wonderful part of bombarding aviation more intimately – attractive from its heroic side and captivating from the impressions it produces; but it is closely linked with another function of war which is even more intimately in touch with battle, and that is night bombardment.

Let us consider the field of activity in this. In modern warfare an immense amount of material is constantly used up and destroyed, and means must be taken to keep up an ample supply in the rear, to be drawn upon as necessary for the troops in the trenches; at the same time it must be out of reach of enemy guns. The artillery has made great progress in this, by increasing the range of their guns and consequently their radius of action, but even then the reserves and material cannot be reached by their cannon. This hammering by enemy guns can only be efficient in the front zone, so that fresh reserves and new material must constantly be brought up.

So this is the business of night bombarding squadrons: to harass the enemy, strike his reserves, cut his lines of communication, set fire to his railroad stations and his aviation hangars, blow up his ammunition depots, fly over his cantonments and bivouacs, flood them with projectiles, decimate the adversary, and deprive him of rest; as a result, on the following day at the hour of attack, we shall find only demoralized troops, without supplies. Between times during fine clear nights, we carry the action farther away. The ammunition factories, foundries, and forges receive a visit from our planes, and a giant charge will result in putting out of use for long months the factories attacked. Still farther, there will be sometimes reprisal raids on the large German cities on the other side of the Rhine.

For these different objects there must be a corresponding means of execution, varying according to the nature of the mission. The light and fast plane will strike the cities which are industrial centres, which distance makes almost invulnerable; and the fighting plane – a big machine – strongly armed, can attack all organizations at the front as well as the factories in the rear. The conditions of adaptation of these planes vary every time, according to the requirements demanded by the proposed objective.

If it is desired to cut lines of communication and interrupt traffic, especially large bombs are dropped from a low altitude and these throw the railroad into such confusion as to require long days of repair. An entire squadron passing over such a place will make such a road totally impassable; or again, it may be individual attacks on running trains followed by derailments, fires, and the stopping of all traffic.

It is desired to destroy ammunition stations? This is a new class of operations; to cover the entire surface of the depot with a great number of small shells, and accomplish its certain destruction by explosion of the shells close to the projectile heaps. On an aerodrome the same tactics are employed, but with incendiary shells, or a few shells of large calibre dropped from a very low height directly upon the hangars. If reserves are seen to be coming, it is necessary to use special shells which burst into an infinite number of pieces, followed by grenades and machine-gun attacks on troops at the disembarking

pier, or farther out on the road leading up to their final positions. Furthermore, machinery of factories cannot escape wrecking from an attack of high-power projectiles dropped upon them.

The diversity of these expeditions, the varying circumstances – always new – in which they are conducted, induce a feeling of fresh interest upon the occasion of every sortie, and offer opportunity to study the methods used, with a view to approaching constantly nearer perfection. It is a strong stimulant for the natural-born bombarder, whose real vocation it is, and who interests himself in his task because conscious of its great power.

How wonderful are the sensations felt in these night flights over the field of battle; lighted by its thousand fuse lights, bursting shells, and the lines of fire of the machine guns; you will remember dear chief, having tasted something of this in the great days of Verdun, where you took part with us in the operations of that time.

It is a spectacle of sublime and savage beauty this – to view a field of carnage by night. When the lines are passed and one engages, in his turn, in the great struggle, surrounded by the illuminating rockets, in the midst of bursting shells, crossed by the searchlight beams searching the heavens with its rays, and to extinguish it with a salvo from a machine gun – to do this without being blinded – then one feels an indescribable joy.

When the end is in sight and the precise moment approaches when the projectiles are to be dropped, one realizes at once the amount of danger that had to be overcome in order to succeed; the fascination of firing, and finally that feeling of strong domination, of superiority over an enemy that one holds at his mercy, and that with a simple turn of the hand he can destroy or save. Such realization awakens the recollection of days gone before, and thrills one with joy in the work of destruction.

An immense field of development opens up before a man in bombarding aviation, and through that, will finally come success. It is a real arm of offensive, and carries the war into the enemy's country. Daily and nightly our colours cross the Rhine and presage the next victory.

Partridge

By the second year of the Great War, one of the German aces, Oswald Boelcke, had so refined the techniques and tactics of fighting in the sky that he was able to produce a handbook, the *Diktat Boelcke*, which set out many of the tactics for aerial combat; these were to hold good for the whole twentieth century and still be taught in the military aviation schools of the twenty-first. The *Diktat* laid down:

Come out of the sun, whenever you can.
Two of you should never attack the same plane – you hazard each other.
If your opponent dives on you, do not evade. Fly to meet him.
Never forget your own line of retreat.

Always try to secure an advantageous position before attacking.
Climb before and during the approach. Dive on him swiftly from above.
Attack when he seems preoccupied with other duties, such as reconnaissance or photography or bombing.
Never try to run away from an enemy fighter. If you are surprised by an enemy on your tail, turn and face him with your guns.
Do not allow the enemy to deceive you. If he seems damaged, follow him down until he crashes, to be sure he is not faking.

Over the next hundred years there were to be a number of notable manuals of aerial combat, including the work of the American General Blesse, written after the Korean War. But the maxims of the *Diktat Boelcke* stood the test of many wars to come.

In the Second World War the speed and power of the planes required even faster reactions, but the principles remained the same. The American pilot John Godfrey, who became one of the noted theorists of air war in the United States, described his first encounter thus:

Breathlessly I saw the 109 between breaks in the cloud as I dove. In diving I had picked up speed and was now doing 550 mph. I was about 500 feet below him and closing fast. Quick now, I've time, I checked all round, in back and above me, to be sure no Germans were doing the same to

Mel Fowler,
Self-portrait in Korea.

me. My speed was slacking off now, but I still had enough to pick up that extra 500 feet and position myself 200 yards dead astern. The 109 was flying straight as an arrow. No weaving. As his plane filled my gunsight, I pressed the trigger.

The Korean War produced aerial contests between an array of different planes, propeller-driven on the North Korean Communist side against the new American jets. But these jets were soon to be challenged by Russian MiGs with even better performance. The painting of Mel Fowler in the cockpit of his jet over Korea is a self portrait. He was a decorated pilot who became a distinguished artist.

Frederic Blesse, who produced his own dicta in *No Guts No Glory*, had more than 600 hours of combat flying in Mustangs and Sabres in both the Korean and Vietnam wars. In the Korean War he was credited with bringing down ten enemy MiGs. He wrote:

This is a story of patience, anxiety, frustration, death, sorrow, and a thousand other words known only to those who day after day fought their way into MiG alley, and back. Each pilot learned something: some learned how to fly. Some learned how to kill. Some learned how to bear sorrow. Some were the finest caliber of fighter pilots our country will ever see.

No Guts No Glory was a treatise of the most detailed manoeuvres required to make a kill, and to avoid being killed.

But behind it all were the twin virtues of aggressiveness and unremitting watchfulness while in the air.

The most influential of theories about war in the air came from an American pilot, John Richard Boyd, who flew Sabres in the Korean War and was subsequently recruited into academe. His *Aerial Attack Study* fundamentally asserted that the awareness and quick thinking of pilots could not only confound enemy aircraft in dogfights, but also evade missiles. Boyd maintained that the pilot in a fight needed to know only two things: the position and the velocity of the enemy. In other words, if he knew what the enemy was capable of, he could plan his own actions.

In an era when it was at one and the same time thought that aerial fighting theory was inordinately complex – with 'scissors', high and low 'yo-yos' and a dozen other manoeuvres – and that dogfighting was a thing of the past, Boyd's clearly expressed theories were adopted and put into full effect in the Gulf War.

He was to extend his advice into overall war planning and was subsequently given credit for a significant contribution to the strategy of the 1991 Gulf War and for the speed with which the morale and the fighting abilities of the Iraqis collapsed.

The Zeppelins

Not since Dutch warships sailed up the Thames estuary in the seventeenth century, had the city of London been threatened by enemy action. Then, within months of the outbreak of

Andrew Carrick Gow, Zeppelin over London.

the Great War, Count Zeppelin's menacing airships were flying over the very centre of the capital and dropping bombs. More than 200 people were killed by them in 1915, while the British struggled to devise a defence against this novel assault. Only one enemy ship was destroyed.

Andrew Carrick Gow's painting depicts what became a macabre spectator sport, as thousands of citizens, alerted by the noisy-engined enemy airships, turned out on to the streets to watch them in their contest with the best efforts of the Royal Flying Corps.

For 1916 had brought the massive new six-engined German craft, designed by the extraordinarily innovative yet practical Count Zeppelin. German propaganda asserted that they could even cross the Atlantic and certainly have the whole of the United Kingdom within range; the cities and arms factories of Britain would be destroyed.

These new airships, with their huge, gas-filled cotton skins, were astonishingly ambitious. They were more than 600ft long, with two gondolas, at front and back, connected by a narrow catwalk, along which the intrepid crew of twenty-three could pass to attend to bombs and machine guns. When the British eventually brought one down, they were amazed by the array of mechanical contrivances which released bombs, controlled flight and operated wireless messages.

The second day of September 1916 saw a great attempt to lay London in ruins. Three of the latest super Zeppelins, accompanied by ten more airships, ranged across the Channel to attack London and the Midland towns.

By now the British had developed powerful searchlights which could reach aircraft even 10,000ft up in the sky. It was also a clear starry night. The newspapers reported that at two in the morning there were tens of thousands of people on the streets of London looking up at the sky. A great airship, in its grey skin, was clearly visible. Then, the papers reported, a faint glow of red showed towards its stern:

It spread with great speed and deepened into a crimson glow, and the whole huge structure began to fall, slowly at first, but gathering momentum and blazing more fiercely as it approached the earth. As the flaming airship fell, high overhead showed other lights from a solitary aeroplane. It was the conqueror in a battle, such as no man before him had ever fought, disclosing his presence in the high air. Not the least astonishing fact about this first encounter in which an airship was brought down on English ground, was that the issue of it was simultaneously known over an area of a thousand square miles, and that the sound of cheering rose in every direction, like the roar of a stormy sea, before the final crash of the fall was heard.

The newspapers soon revealed that the hero of the hour was Lieutenant W. L. Robinson of the Royal Flying Corps, who had been patrolling for some hours before he saw the Zeppelin and attacked it.

Robinson landed safely and, cold and exhausted though he was, was bundled into a car and driven straight to Cuffley, near Potters Bar in Hertfordshire, where the Zeppelin had come down. The papers reported that, by then, 60,000 spectators had gathered at the site, and they gave Robinson a

Sir John Lavery,
Convoy off the
Baltic Coast.

prolonged and rapturous reception. He was to be awarded the Victoria Cross.

One German Zeppelin commander gave a jaunty description to an American newspaper correspondent of what it was like to be attacking the city:

> London is darkened but sufficiently lighted for me to see its reflected glow in the sky from nearly forty miles away. It is a fairylike picture. There is no sign of life, excepting in the distance a moving light, probably from a railway train. As in the twinkling of an eye, all this changes. A sudden flash and a beam of brilliant light reaches out from below and begins to feel around the sky. Soon there are more than a score of criss-crossing ribbons seeking to drag us to destruction.

This was Commander Mathy. He claimed to have reached the centre of the city:

> Mingling with the dim thunder from the guns below came the explosions and bursting flames of our bombs. Over Holborn Viaduct we dropped several bombs. From the Bank of England to the Tower, I tried to hit the bridge and believe I was successful. Over Liverpool Street station I shouted 'Rapid fire!' and bombs rained down. I could see that I hit well and apparently did great damage.

Mathy's wishful bravado came to an end with the destruction of his own airship at the beginning of October 1916, when it succumbed to an aircraft attack and fell only a few miles away from the first crash site in Potters Bar. By the end of 1916, the British had accounted for eight Zeppelins, including one which came down almost intact in Essex, its crew safely clambering out and surrendering to a policeman. The Zeppelin crisis was over.

But for that year or two early in the Great War the airship had seemed the most useful, as well as the most devastating, invention of the time. Its speed, endurance and capacity to reach great heights had made it seem almost invulnerable, until the new tactics of the Royal Flying Corps eventually came into effect. The towns and cities of the Midlands and the English east coast were victims of attack as the great ships slid across their territory – Yorkshire, Norfolk, even, in dire anticipation of things to come in another war, Coventry.

But the airships and the Zeppelins had another great use, as 'eyes in the sky'.

The German commanders at the naval battle of Jutland attributed their success in escaping from Beatty and Jellicoe's battleships in no small way to the information sent down to them from the sky about the movements of the British fleet.

Sir John Lavery's painting of a convoy heading north was a tribute to the valuable information that the airships could give to troops or sailors confined to ground and sea level.

Bombers and Fighters

By the third year of the war, although the Germans were building even more massive airships, their strategy turned to attacking London with the new Gotha bomber aircraft. Zeppelins were still used, including the larger new version.

Louis Weirter, An Aerial Fight.

But the Gothas proved they could reach, identify, and strike targets in London. When the Gothas first appeared, the British air command put together a force of almost a hundred planes to take them on. But the existing fighters could not match the Gothas for speed, altitude or rate of climb, and the Germans found themselves able to attack London almost with impunity. By the middle of 1917, the Gothas were able to bomb Shoeburyness, Harwich and even central London. The loss of a hundred children when a nursery was hit, and another hundred young naval recruits at a training establishment greatly intensified people's fear of bombardment. Yet of twenty or more Gothas involved in these early raids, all but one or two returned to their bases unscathed.

However, British aircraft designers were also developing new weapons. The Sopwith Camel, introduced in 1917, showed that it was capable of severely damaging the Gotha formations during their daylight raids – forcing the Germans to switch to night-time. But it was not until early 1918 that the British night fighters managed to actually shoot down a Gotha, and only after a string of damaging night attacks on central London, including on Chelsea and Long Acre.

Zeppelin attacks continued even as the Allies in France were pushing the Germans towards defeat. In August 1918 a Zeppelin was shot down by British fighters over the North Sea – the last airship to attempt a raid on Britain.

The Aces

Louis Weirter's picture, An Aerial Fight, may be unique in all of art.

The painter, as he told his sister Caroline, actually witnessed this supreme deed of valour which was to end in the supreme recognition of courage, the Victoria Cross. The picture indeed has a splendid ring of authenticity, the pursuing aircraft hurtling through the clouds to close in on the Royal Flying Corps plane.

Weirter was an observer in a balloon on 2 June 1917, when he witnessed the Great War's ultimate air ace, Billy Bishop, encounter this quartet of German planes, which he was to defeat and destroy. Bishop was returning from a solo raid on a German airfield, where he had destroyed a number of enemy aircraft on the ground, when he ran into German fighters. He was awarded the Victoria Cross, the following month, for this outstanding act of courage.

Bishop, a Canadian who survived the war and went on to become a senior Air Force officer, was officially credited with seventy-two victories in the Great War, more than any other British, American or Empire ace. He became a specialist in 'lone wolf' attacks on objectives behind the German lines. On one occasion he was forced to crash-land only 300 yards from the German trenches, but was able to get out of his machine and run to the Allied lines.

Before the June exploit, Bishop had already, the previous month, been awarded the Distinguished Service Order for shooting down two aircraft while being attacked by four others. He was later to destroy the German air ace, Paul Billik, and his victorious career continued through 1918.

Louis Weirter was a Scotsman, from Edinburgh, who became an official war artist. His painting of the Battle of Courcellette, with its shattered guns, aircraft in the sky and

Alphonse Jongers, Portrait of Billy Bishop.

tanks being used for the first time in France, depicted the devastated strongpoint which the Canadians captured during the Battle of the Somme in 1916. It was much reproduced. Weirter was actually present here too, as a soldier, when the battle was fought.

Jongers' portrait of Bishop in full dress parades perhaps the ultimate array of medals from the Great War. There is the Victoria Cross, the Distinguished Service Order – awarded twice, indeed – the Distinguished Flying Cross, the Military Cross. From the French he received the Croix de Guerre and the Legion of Honour.

It was already March 1917 when Bishop first arrived in France flying the Nieuport 17 with 60 Squadron. The action in which Weirter saw him earn him his VC was one of the victories which Bishop was able to claim in only sixty days of actual combat flying on the Western Front. The citation for his Distinguished Flying Cross read:

A most successful and fearless fighter in the air, he has rendered signally valuable services in personally destroying twenty five enemy machines in twelve days, five of which he destroyed on the last day of his service at the front. His value as a moral factor to the Royal Air Force cannot be over-estimated.

It was this value which saw Bishop summoned back to a great welcome in Canada. He eventually reached the rank of Air Marshal and was to remain a key public figure for the Canadian Air Force right through a second war.

Arnold's picture of a dogfight, with one fatally damaged aircraft collapsing down to earth, records the death of the most famous British pilot of the Great War, Captain Albert Ball VC.

Arnold had himself been a pilot and survived a number of encounters with enemy aircraft. Ball, who had by then been credited with downing forty-four German aircraft, ran into a flight of Germans, including one of the Richthofen brothers – known as the Red Baron. Ball's death, when he was still only twenty years old, was finally acknowledged by the British a month later, when he received his posthumous VC, and the British press published extensive tributes. Trenchard, the Royal Flying Corps chief, said it was 'the greatest loss the Corps could sustain at that time'.

A Nottingham teenager when war broke out, Ball had first joined up in one of the curious Cycling Regiments. But when he could not get the transfer he wanted to the Royal Flying Corps, he paid privately to be taught to fly. This sufficed for him then to be accepted by the RFC.

He went to France, within a month survived being shot down by anti-aircraft fire and flew nearly all the different aircraft then in use. He perfected a strategy whereby, with a machine gun mounted on the wing above him, he would come up underneath an enemy plane and fire into its belly. His red-painted propeller hub became as celebrated as the livery of the Red Baron.

Cecil Lewis, who had gone straight from Oundle School into the Royal Flying Corps as a seventeen-year-old, was in Ball's squadron on his final flight. Poet and writer as he was to become, Lewis described that fateful day:

Norman G. Arnold, The Last Flight of Captain Ball.

The squadron sets out eleven strong on the evening patrol. Eleven chocolate-coloured, lean, noisy bullets, lifting, swaying, turning, rising into formation. They are off to deal with Richthofen and his circus of Red Albatrosses. The May evening is heavy with threatening masses of cumulus cloud, majestic skyscapes, solid looking as snow mountains, fraught with caves and valleys, rifts and ravines – strange and secret pathways in the chartless continents of the sky. Steadily the body of scouts rises higher and higher, threading its way between the cloud precipices. Sometimes, below, the streets of a village, the corner of a wood, a few dark figures moving.

But the fighting pilot's eyes are not on the ground, but roving endlessly through the lower and higher reaches of the sky, peering anxiously through fur goggles to spot those black slow-moving specks against land or cloud which mean full throttle, tense muscles, held breath and the headlong plunge with screaming wires – a Hun in the sights and tracer flashing. A red light curls up from the leader's cockpit. He has seen six scouts three thousand feet below. Black crosses. The pilots nurse their engines, hard-minded and set, test their guns. At last the leader sways sideways, as a signal that each should take his man. And suddenly drops. Machines fall scattering, the earth races up, the enemy patrol, startled, wheels and breaks. Each his man. A burst, fifty rounds – it is over. They have overshot. But our squadron, plunging into action, had not seen, far off, approaching from the east the rescue flight of Red Albatrosses. The British scouts, engaging and disengaging like flies at midday in a summer room, soon find the newcomers upon them. Then, as if attracted by some mysterious power, other bodies of machines swoop down from the peaks of the cloud mountains.

A pilot, in the seconds between his own engagements, might see a Hun diving vertically, an SE 5 on his tail, on the tail of the SE another Hun, and above him again another British scout. These four, plunging headlong at two hundred miles an hour, guns crackling, tracer streaming, suddenly break up. The lowest Hun plunges flaming to his death. The victor seems to stagger, suddenly pulls out in a great leap, as a trout leaps on the end of a line, and then, turning over on his belly, swoops and spins in a dizzy falling spiral, with the earth to end it.

Such a glimpse, lasting perhaps ten seconds, is broken by the sharp rattle of another attack. Two machines approach head-on at breakneck speed, firing at each other. Who will hold longest? They fling their machines sideways, bank and circle, each striving to bring his gun onto the other's tail.

But from above, this strange tormented circling is seen by another Hun. He drops. His gun speaks. The British machine falls bottom uppermost down through the clouds and the deep unending desolation of the twilight sky.

As Lewis and the remaining planes make for home, he cannot resist a peroration:

In the pellucid sky, serene cloud mountains mass and move unceasingly. Here where guns rattled and death plucked the spirits of the valiant, this thing is now as if it had never been. The sky is busy with night, passive, superb, unheeding.

However, he returns to a grimmer canvas:

Of the eleven scouts that went out that evening, only five of us returned to the aerodrome.

Ball never returned. I believe I was the last to see him in his red nosed SE going east at eight thousand feet. He flew straight into the white face of an enormous cloud. I followed, but when I came out on the other side, he was nowhere to be seen.

William T. Wood was the official war artist appointed to the Balkans, and these paintings were made in the final stages of the war on the Salonika front.

The balloons, tethered by a wire to a winch mounted on a lorry, could stay aloft watching enemy activity for many hours. Below the gas-filled envelope hung a precarious-looking basket containing, usually, a couple of crew engaged in spotting targets for the heavy guns below. Their steady position, despite being buffeted by both winds and enemy artillery, was nevertheless the most effective way of registering the accuracy of guns which had a range of ten miles or more, far beyond anything that could be seen at ground level. Messages down the wire from the balloonist could correct the guns' aim with unique precision.

But to the other side, both on the ground and in the air, these envelopes of flammable gas were the most tempting of targets. Pilots in all air forces became expert balloon-busters. The balloons had no significant defences, but they were close enough to the ground to make flying at them especially hazardous for an attacker.

One balloonist described watching a German plane take out four nearby balloons with tracer bullets: 'First there were great clouds of black smoke, then the flames, and then the balloon dropped exactly like a burning paper bag.'

The balloonists, however, had one lifeline which no other airmen enjoyed. They had parachutes. The 'chute was attached to the basket, so that when the balloonist jumped out it automatically opened – a ripcord effect – and usually delivered its wearer safely to the ground. The balloonists' right to escape seems to have been regarded by those below with an element of knightly chivalry. Indeed, when a British airman offended against the code, on a bright day with thousands of witnesses, he was, it seems, greeted with opprobrium. By his own account, he shot up a balloon, then saw the observer parachute out:

The balloon itself is only rubber and silk filled with gas, comparatively valueless and easily replaceable. But the observer is a trained man who has sat in that balloon basket day after day, knows the layout of our trenches, and has probably spotted most of our artillery positions. His knowledge is of value to the enemy and he is not easily replaceable. Therefore I followed him down as he swung helplessly below his parachute and shot the best part of a hundred rounds into him, or around him, which I do not know, as his body just continued to swing.

Leonard Bridgman's painting was based on a personal account which Bert Hall gave him of his first experience of what was known to pilots as 'balloon jumping', regarded as a particularly hazardous operation. Hall had, by 1916, joined the Escadrille Lafayette, a squadron of flyers made up of American volunteers. He and his friend Nimmie Prince – his plane armed with six sky rockets – were ordered up to attack a balloon. Hall recounted:

It was a perfectly clear day, and we went as high as our Nieuports would carry us so as to fool the German observers as long as possible, before we nosed over and started diving. A balloon job is either a success or a failure the very first time you try, as the crew on the ground haul in their 'sausage' at the first note of warning from the observers. In this case we were diving with the sun at our backs and were not observed until we had gained great speed. When at last the warning was given and the ground crew began to haul in the cable, every anti-aircraft gun in the neighbourhood opened up. It was a veritable hail storm of bullets. Down, down, down we went until we were in range of the great lumbering gas bag. The reeling-in speed of the balloon was of course nothing to the speed of our dive. All of a sudden a streak of fire shot ahead of us. It was Nimmie's sky rockets. They seemed to land in the very middle of the balloon. Then I saw both German observers go over the side. The next moment, their parachutes opened and they sailed down to safety. .

As I pulled away, a long column of fire shot skyward. I saw the fabric on my centre section was badly frazzled.

The anti-aircraft fire and machine gunning that I had been through had riddled my plane. I landed back without mishap. But when my plane rolled to a stop the wings collapsed around me as if they were made of cardboard.

There was considerable celebration over our first balloon. Nimmie had a long conversation with someone at headquarters. He finally convinced them that balloons could be moved, and could also be shot down if the pilots had guts enough and didn't mind flying in a barrage as thick as pea soup.

The fact that parachutes were of proven value but were only issued to the balloonists was, both during and after the war, a subject of gloomy speculation among the men who flew the planes. Many flyers had seen their comrades shot down, tumbling out of the sky, often bursting into flame. Some reported having seen the pilot or observer deliberately jump out of a burning plane, opting for the certain death of impact on the ground rather than endure the flames.

The talk in the squadron messes was that the authorities believed that issuing parachutes might make pilots less brave – that they might prefer to abandon a plane that was damaged but might still have made a landing.

After the war, one pilot, Arthur Gould Lee, who went on to become an Air Vice-Marshal in the RAF, decided to investigate. He refuted any suggestion that the practicality of using parachutes in aircraft was unproven. In 1912 there had been a successful free-fall jump from a Wright aeroplane in the United States, and the same year, there was a

William T. Wood,
Balloonists parachuting.

Roland Pitchforth, Parachutist.

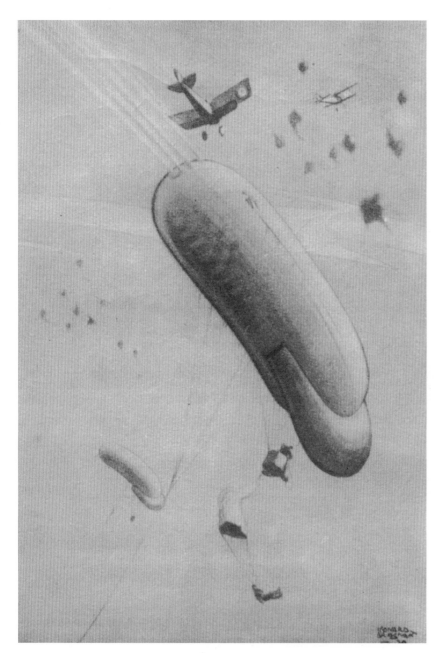 

Leonard Bridgman, Attack on a Balloon (left) and Dogfight (right).

demonstration at Hendon airfield in the UK. Gould Lee was able, after the war, to search the archives, where he found no evidence of what he called 'the grave calumny' that parachutes were denied to British airmen because it would encourage the abandonment of aircraft; nor had Trenchard, head of the RAF, ever expressed any similar view.

But Gould Lee did catalogue the continuing failure on the part of the British authorities to encourage the development of parachutes, or even to follow up work that had been done by private individuals. A British civilian engineer, E. R. Calthrop, had developed a design which, six months before the war, had already been successfully tested, with the help of the Vickers armaments manufacturer at Barrow-in-Furness in Lancashire. In fact, Gould Lee's researches revealed that there had been a catalogue of attempts, right through the war, to develop Calthrop's design. A Royal Aircraft Factory superintendent, Mervyn O'Gorman, tried, in the autumn of 1915, to get permission from the Director of Military Armaments for trials, but Gould Lee found a peremptory note of reply from the Director, General Henderson, to this request: 'No. Certainly not!'

Calthrop and his supporters tried, throughout the war, to gain official support for their work. Gould Lee finally opined that it was the sheer ignorance of combat flying amongst the upper echelons of the Royal Flying Corps – one senior officer wrote that crippled aircraft simply fell too fast for the crew to get out – that blocked development of the device which, it is now calculated, has saved at least a quarter of a million airmen's lives.

Air and the Empire

Tony Theobald's picture is of an aircraft which had arrived and acquitted itself well on the Western Front in the last months of the Great War and was to prove a key link in the development of the RAF. In one celebrated instance in August 1918, Lieutenant Spurling, flying a DH9, had found himself facing thirty Fokkers. He shot down five of them and still managed to get home.

With the ending of the First World War, and suffering a notable shortage of money, Britain found herself with a plethora of continuing challenges, both within the existing Empire and in the territories she had acquired or had had bestowed on her by the peace treaties.

Somaliland and the lands of the Upper Nile had been troublesome for thirty years or more. It was pertinent, then, that the post-war Secretary of State for Defence and Air in 1919 was none other than Winston Churchill, who had personally taken part in the Sudan campaign of the 1890s to subdue the followers of the Mahdi, the so-called Dervishes; indeed, he wrote a vivid account in his book *The River War* of the great cavalry charge which he had participated in at the Battle of Omdurman.

Twenty years on, a rebellion by the so-called Mad Mullah and his Dervishes was threatening British interests and resources in Somaliland. Churchill was aware that it might cost millions to send ground troops to deal with them, and he seems to have been easily persuaded by Trenchard that the new Royal Air Force and its DH9 bombers could do the job a lot more quickly and cheaply.

Thus a mere dozen de Havilland DH9s were put on board HMS *Ark Royal* and shipped to Suez. In January 1920 they bombed the Dervish capital, Taleh, killing the Mullah's main commander and a number of the Mullah's family; the Mullah himself escaped to the hills, while Britain's Somaliland Camel Corps moved in to take control. This was the last that was seen of the Dervish rebellion.

Churchill, told that the whole affair had only cost about a quarter of a million pounds, seems to have been converted to Trenchard's assertion that the RAF and its planes could be the core of a new and economical means of putting down resistance in various parts of the Empire. Mesopotamia, the new British mandate, duly became the home of RAF squadrons, accompanied by the artist brothers Sydney and Richard Carline.

The Carline Brothers

The Carlines were to have a huge artistic success in their London exhibitions after the war, particularly with their canvases of the action in Mesopotamia. But they had both seen plenty of action on the Western Front and then, in Sydney's case, in the closing months of the war, when the Austrians were driven out of Italy.

Sydney Carline's paintings reflect just how personal fighting in the sky could be. In a letter home, early in Sydney's time in France, he described attacking a German reconnaissance plane which was taking photographs below him over the Allied lines: 'We dived on him. He put up no show. The pilot was shot and the observer leaning over tried to dive for home, but he was also shot and the machine crashed in the river.'

After the war he was to recall these and other encounters with less relish, commenting to a newspaper interviewer in 1927 that he often pondered on the people he had killed in his years of combat flying. Around that time, his wife Gwendolyn reported that he showed quite serious symptoms of depression when he talked about his flying career.

From the start, his combat and action paintings reflect the joy, wonderment and fascination he experienced in flying through the clouds, gazing at sunrises and sunsets and seeing the landscape stretched out below and beyond, whether in France, the Italian Alps or the deserts and hills of Mesopotamia. The triumphant excitement of diving downwards, in his picture of an attack on an Austrian airfield at Sacile, resonates across the canvas.

When he could, he made pencil sketches while actually flying. This was a hazardous policy. More than once he was surprised by German or Austrian planes hurtling down at him from the very cloudscape he was trying to sketch. But his notable flying skills and the manoeuvrability of his Sopwith Camel plane saved the day each time. His picture of planes and aircraft fire over the Alps shows the detail he was aiming at. Within half an hour or so of landing he made a point of trying to render his work in water colour. Spurring his Camel upwards across the Alpine sky gave him, he said, 'an exhilaration like nothing on earth'. The vertiginous painting of British planes over a little Italian town in the Alps revels in those sensations which were to infuse his work throughout his Air Force career.

Tony Theobald, DH9 Biplane.

It was in early 1919 that the Imperial War Museum, conscious that its mission to reflect the Great War in art had struggled to encompass the new experience of war in the air, decided to dispatch the Carlines to Mesopotamia. The brothers were to bring back not only evocations of combat in the skies, but also a panoply of new and exhilarating canvases depicting the British Empire's lately acquired territory, the pattern and palette of its landscape, the scenes of history and of conflicts remote, recent and ongoing, and the broad expanses of the biblical lands, from the Jordan to the Tigris and Galilee.

The paintings they brought back were vivid testimony to the new opportunities that eyes from the sky could bring to the realities of conquering the Empire as well as astonishing the earthbound artistic world.

Mesopotamia – known today as Iraq – was bestowed, along with Palestine, as what were termed Mandates, on Britain by the Versailles peace conference, after much discussion about what to do with the remnants of the defeated Ottoman Empire. The British were anyway in effective occupation of Mesopotamia after General Allenby's push all the way up from the Suez Canal to occupy Damascus. But an array of promises had been made to the Arabs in the area – notably by T. E. Lawrence – that in return for joining the Allies against the Turks they would have their independence.

The concept of the Mandate was ultimately invented to acknowledge the realities of power on the ground – the French received Mandates in Syria and Lebanon – while giving some authority to the local Arab chiefs. British officials and politicians largely regarded Mesopotamia and Palestine, and the Mandates, as simply additions to the British Empire. But the proposals at the peace conference were contested by numerous groups within the area of what was to be the Mandate territory, and riots and rebellions broke out.

The British government, already beset at home by economic, financial, and industrial problems, was reluctant to commit more troops and resources to subduing discontent in its new and turbulent territory. Winston Churchill, however, as Colonial Secretary, was determined to assert his department's leading role in Mesopotamia. He was well aware of the cost of keeping troops in the Mandate territory and, after the experience of Sudan and Somaliland, was already advocating that air power, combined with very mobile armoured cars, would suffice to snuff out the various trouble-makers. And so, largely, it proved.

It was this early post-war scenario that provided the Carline brothers with the chance to make their unique contribution. They contrived to get lifts in the second seats of Australian Air Force planes, even sometimes flying them themselves, and were taken on missions against Arab rebels, Kurds and mutinying troops.

Richard's painting of Baghdad in 1919, a key city in the new Empire, was a most emphatic assertion of what the new view from the sky could deliver, with the river dark and restrained as it passes through the centre of the city and then bursting into exuberant blue as it snakes out through the countryside. The density of the city, compressed by the desert

Sydney Carline, Scouts over Asiago.

Sydney Carline, Attack on an
Airfield at Sacile.

Sydney Carline, Anti-aircraft Fire over Piave.

against the river banks, is eloquent elucidation of travellers' reports on the ground of intensely crowded, sometimes almost impassable, streets, and teeming humanity.

His painting of Jerusalem looking towards the Dead Sea, with its walls tightly encompassing the assertively differentiated quarters, gives a picture of that most holy of cities which could only have been imagined by Christians, Muslims and Jews from Crusader times right up to the recent war. The Golden Temple has its select position, along with the old fort.

The picture of Kut al-Amara resurrects the deadly story of what had happened there just four years before the Carlines arrived in Mesopotamia. This was the scene of one of the worst military disasters the British had ever experienced up to that time. General Townshend had retreated from the gates of Baghdad, then took the calamitous decision to make a stand at Kut, before surrendering, after a long siege by the Turks. Thousands of his troops died of thirst, hunger and disease as they were marched across the desert to captivity in Turkey.

Again, it is the bold strokes of the landscape seen from the air which dominate, with the loop of the River Tigris defining Carline's picture. The action above the landscape is, of course, retrospective, with a German or Turkish plane perhaps diving to intercept the Allied aircraft, of which we see only one wing.

The fall of Kut had come in 1915 and, as a piece of historical painting of the fortress which was to become part of the new Empire, it is arguably quite accurate. When the Ottomans entered the war, less than a year earlier, they had no Air Force at all. Their new allies, the Germans, had set about plugging this gap by breaking down some planes into small pieces so that they could be shipped east on railway wagons. Despite attempts to disguise this unusual freight, the first three trains were stopped and the parts confiscated in Bulgaria, still neutral at the time. But in early 1915 four of the next railway-borne aircraft did get through and, by March 1915, were flying, with German pilots. Their most urgent task had been to help confront the British forces making their way up the Tigris. Then the planes were taken to pieces again and, in a nine-week-long epic journey, transported by river raft, horse-drawn wagon, even camel, to the front line. They eventually arrived at Kut to add to the pressure which finally forced Townshend to concede defeat.

It is, perhaps, permissible in such lethal times as our own, to think of Richard Carline's painting of Samarra as depicting not only an island in the desert, but also, as in the ancient Mesopotamian legend, the place of an appointment with death.

His picture of Gaza, a city now, a hundred years on, associated in the contemporary mind with death, confrontation and devastation, is an appealing rendering of a prosperous and peaceful town, with a myriad shades of green fertility surrounding a meticulously laid out array of streets. There is a grand-looking temple, a high road, minutely cultivated inner fields. Gaza had in fact been at the centre of the British Army's advance through Palestine, with cavalry charges and fierce fighting, only two years earlier. But Carline's aerial depiction suggests an almost perfect idyll. The Carline brothers were to go on to paint an impressive array of pictures of this latest territory that Britain's Empire had acquired.

Richard Carline, Baghdad.

Richard Carline, Jerusalem and the Dead Sea.

Richard Carline, Siege of Kut al-Amara Seen from the Air.

Sydney Carline was perhaps the first artist to try to encompass the actual experience of flying, not only in combat, but in the sense of relishing independence from the earth below, enveloping body and mind in the changing atmosphere of cloud and then the purest clarity of desert sunshine. His painting of flying over the desert is unalloyed joy. He is above the setting sun, with a river and an inland sea below. His Flying above Kirkuk, looking back over the tail of his aircraft with three other planes dancing behind, evokes not only the wind in the wires, but also the superlative confidence with which the flyers whirled their machines about the sky.

In his pictures of record, like that of the Wadi Fara Gorge, where a large contingent of Turkish troops were trapped and destroyed, the aircraft always have the prime position. But Wadi Fara already had a special place as the first engagement, in Palestine at least, where victory was obtained primarily by air power. General Allenby reported that his airmen not only dropped bombs on the enemy but hit them with their machine guns from lower altitudes. As Allenby said, 'The roads by which the Turks were trying to flee were, in consequence, littered and choked with dead men and dead horses, smashed guns and wrecked transport of all kinds.'

Sydney Carline's painting, done, as he said, after he had made several flights over the Gorge, shows with unforgettable clarity the narrowness and steepness of the Gorge, which contributed to such a devastating Turkish debacle. Within a month the Turks were suing for peace.

Sydney Carline described a flight they made over Jerusalem, only to see quite clearly that there were crowds gathering menacingly down below. He and his brother airmen decided to perform a long series of aerial stunts over the city, which, according to Sydney, sufficed to distract the crowds below, and allowed the authorities on the ground to regain some control.

When they were flying with the Australian Air Force over the Kurdish areas, they were quickly made aware of the hazards below. What looked like an idyllic oasis – and the brothers were truly beguiled by the beauty of Palestine and Arabia – turned out to be occupied by hostile tribesmen, who turned their rifles on them and started shooting. Sydney recorded, laconically, that they were fortunately not very good shots.

When his paintings were shown in London, visitors and critics were agog at the beauty and originality of the aerial views of Mesopotamia. They had quite simply seen nothing like them. Sydney explained that he had done the drawings for them actually while flying in slow downward circles repeatedly over the landscapes which attracted him. The critics acclaimed these as the first paintings done by a pilot in flight – although, of course, the Frenchman Henri Farré had done something similar quite early in the war. But this show made Sydney's reputation, and he was consequently invited to take up the post of Master of Drawing at Ruskin College, Oxford.

Richard Carline, The City of Samarra.

Richard Carline, Gaza.

Sydney Carline, Flying over the Desert at Sunset.

Sydney Carline, Flying above Kirkuk.

Sydney Carline,
Destruction of the
Turkish Transport.

Bombing the Cities

Pablo Picasso created his huge painting of Guernica in 1937 in the wake of what *The Times* correspondent George Steer described as an air attack 'unparalleled in military history'. The painting is a panorama of agony, with the grieving and the screaming women and the soldier lying with his shattered sword beneath an impaled horse, the marks of stigmata on his hand. It was shown first in Paris, then exhibited across Europe and the United States, and many people saw it as a dreadful portent of what war from the air might bring.

Steer arrived in Guernica a few hours after the bombing:

At 2.00 a.m. today when I visited the town, the whole of it was a horrible sight, flaming from end to end. Throughout the night houses were falling, until the streets became long heaps of red impenetrable debris. Carts piled high with such household possessions as could be saved from the conflagration clogged the roads all night. Round the burning town other survivors were lying on mattresses or looking for lost relatives or children.

Steer was able to put together the details of how this first major example of what became known as carpet bombing had been achieved. It was about 4.30 in the afternoon of Monday, a market day, when a single German bomber appeared and dropped six bombs and grenades, which were apparently aimed at the railway station but hit a number of houses. It was followed by a second bomber, whose load hit the middle of the town. The planes involved were Junkers and Heinkels.

After these two early strikes, Steer was told, three Junkers arrived together, and thereafter, in Steer's words, the bombing grew in intensity, ceasing only with the approach of dusk:

The whole town was systematically pounded to pieces. All the villages around were bombed with the same intensity. At Mujica, a little group of houses at the head of the inlet, the population was machine-gunned for fifteen minutes.

Steer's assessment of this attack was clear: 'The object of the bombardment was seemingly the demoralization of the civil population.' He then offered a judgement 'which may be of interest to students of the new military science':

First, small parties of aeroplanes threw heavy bombs, choosing area after area in orderly fashion. Next came fighting machines, which swooped low to machine-gun those who ran in panic from their shelters. The object of this move was apparently to drive the population underground again as next, twelve bombers at a time appeared dropping heavy and incendiary bombs upon the ruins to wreck the houses and burn them on top of their victims.

Hospitals and all but one of the churches were destroyed, Steer recorded.

The Spanish Civil War had already become a proving ground for new aircraft. Franco's Nationalist rebels had Junkers planes with which they airlifted large numbers of troops from Morocco to southern Spain. Mussolini sent Fiat planes to Franco, and Hitler sent Messerschmitts.

The Republican side received from the Soviet Union the Polikarpov monoplane, designed and built in one of Stalin's gulag factories and outperforming, though not outnumbering, some of the Nationalist planes.

Göring and the other Luftwaffe leaders were thus given a unique lesson in the likely tactics of yet another war.

Picasso, Guernica.

Part II

The Second World War

The New War

The Second World War was scarcely two months old when the British public were confronted with a picture on the cover of the magazine *War Illustrated* which gave a glimpse of the threat from the skies which was to cause terror to so many residents of British cities. It was a crashed German plane shot down in Scotland.

Inside was the story of the RAF pilot Peter Ayerst, who had flown his Hurricane into Germany in November 1939 and found himself the target of an overwhelming posse of enemy aircraft. He was chasing a German reconnaissance aircraft, crossed the border and found himself joining up with a Messerschmitt formation. He rapidly turned and fled, pursued by what turned out to be twenty-seven German planes. Fortuitously, Ayerst then ran into a French squadron, who swooped on the chasing planes and brought nine of them down.

Confusion about what enemy planes looked like in the air was one of the frequent hazards that confronted the pilots of the RAF, particularly in the early months of the war. In 1940, as the Germans swept through Belgium and France towards Dunkirk, they were able to put into the skies an array of aircraft which the RAF men had never seen.

Wing Commander Donaldson sternly advised his air crews, 'It's obviously no good if you are going up to fight the enemy if you cannot at once recognize an aircraft to be friend or foe.' He recounted his own experience over Dunkirk:

I was patrolling the beaches and had notification that some British bombers would be returning through my area, and would I keep a friendly eye on them.

After a while, seven Bristol Blenheims appeared out of the smoke of Dunkirk. To my horror, I noticed they were closely followed by seven twin-engine German fighters, ME 110s.

So I detailed seven of my fighters to accompany me, and we went in behind the MEs. I was about to open fire on the leading ME when the rear gunner started to wave at me. I immediately saw that the MEs were in fact British Hampden bombers, which are quite similar, both having double rudders. I ordered my squadron to break away at once without firing. But then the MEs decided we were the enemy. A terrific fight ensued. We shot down three of them. But afterwards we were able to work out what had probably happened. The MEs had obviously got orders to escort seven of their Junkers 88s on their

Paul Nash, Whitley Bombers over Berlin.

way to bomb our shipping in the Channel, and having seen seven bombers, had formed up to escort them, These were actually the Bristol Blenheims, which look not dissimilar to the Junkers. When we arrived, they must have mistaken us for ME109s, which had probably been detailed to escort them. So there were the Blenheims being escorted by MEs, who were being escorted by Hurricanes.

You can see these mistakes in identity do happen. And are really serious.

For readers of *War Illustrated*, the *Daily Mail* and other papers, all this was a stark reminder of the size of the air power which was being brought to bear, even in those first weeks, only a few miles away on the other side of the Channel.

Ayerst, already a fighter pilot before war broke out, was to survive not only the Battle of Britain and other campaigns but live to become a senior RAF officer and test pilot.

Paul Nash's painting of Whitley bombers over Berlin is an appreciation of the only night bomber which the RAF had in service at the beginning of the war; also, perhaps, a reminder of their first distinctive exploit. On the night that war was declared, they were dispatched to bomb Germany, not with explosives, but with propaganda leaflets. There is no record of the effect of this raid on the, one must presume, bemused populace.

In fact, by the time the Whitleys came out of front-line service, more than 1,800 of them had been built and they had delivered nearly 10,000 tons of bombs on Germany and Occupied Europe, for the loss of 269 planes in action.

The Battle of Britain

The Battle of Britain took place across the summer of 1940. It was Hitler's attempt to establish air supremacy before his planned invasion of England, Operation Sea Lion.

For a time, in the last week of August and the first week of September, it was a damned close-run thing. The RAF was losing pilots and planes faster than they could be replaced. They lost nearly 500 Spitfires and Hurricanes, while fewer than 300 arrived from the factories. More than 200 pilots were killed or wounded out of a total strength of fewer than 1,000.

At the same time, Britain was facing huge formations of German bombers targeting RAF airfields and aircraft factories. Two hundred bombers took part in a raid on the Dunlop tyre factory in Birmingham, and the RAF station at Biggin Hill was bombed out of operation, though only for a matter of hours.

The contest in the skies was testing the capabilities of the Spitfires and the Hurricanes and their pilots to the limit. But they did have some unique advantages.

William T. Rawlinson's picture shows the mysterious – at least to the Germans – steel towers which appeared around the east coast of England in the last months before the war. Indeed, the Germans dispatched a series of Zeppelins in the summer of 1939 to cruise up and down the North Sea and the Channel and try to make sense of the radio signals which were emanating from these constructions.

Fortunately, they did not succeed. And the Chain Home radars survived, their true significance to be realized a year

Barnett Freedman, Aircraft runway being constructed at Thélus, near Arras, May 1940.

William T. Rawlinson, Chain Radar.

later when they became absolutely crucial to the outcome of the Battle of Britain by delivering early warning of impending Luftwaffe attacks, allowing the RAF to get their planes in the air and at the right place, before the attacking bombers and fighters could reach much further than the Channel.

Chain Home was one of the super-secret scientific developments which had been supported by the British Government and the armed forces almost as soon as the Nazi threat became clear. Men who were to become celebrated after the war, like Robert Watson Watt in radar and Professor R. V. Jones with his foil deception device on D-Day, were working on the most advanced techniques from the mid-1930s.

Watson Watt and his colleague, Arnold Wilkins, began work on what would become Chain Home in 1935, when they were asked to look at whether death rays, much featured in the films of the time, could actually be a reality. Indeed, a prize was actually offered to anyone who could produce a ray that would kill a sheep at 100 yards. No one managed to claim it. But Watson Watt and Wilkins were already aware that the reflection of radio waves could act as a measure of distance from the transmitter. By 1937 they had produced a specification which allowed assessment not only of distance but also of height, and were able to show the authorities, and Winston Churchill, that it actually worked. The construction of Chain Home began, and made its crucial contribution in 1940.

The Germans were aware that the masts must be making some contribution to their failures to overcome the RAF and did attack some of them. But rapid repair and a strategy of changing frequencies meant that they never appreciated what Chain Home was doing, and the system survived to demonstrate for the first time the power of early warning radar.

Indeed, the Battle of Britain ace, Wing Commander Johnny Johnson, was convinced that the Chain Home radars were actually the critical difference in the battle. Germany, he wrote, had the planes, the aircrews and the opportunity to win the battle:

> But Göring went about it the wrong way. He should have put out the eyes of Fighter Command by destroying the nineteen radar stations between the Wash and the Isle of Wight, have destroyed RAF fighters by strafing them on the ground, and their communications by bombing. Simultaneously with the radar attacks, the six fighter airfields near the coast between Tangmere and the Thames, the five sector stations near London and the headquarters of Fighter Command at Bentley Priory and Uxbridge should have been struck. Small, compact formations should have attacked these thirty-two targets two or three times a day, until reconnaissance showed that further blows were unnecessary.

Rawlinson, the Chain Home artist, was a Liverpool school teacher who had volunteered for the RAF at the beginning of the war and had actually served with a radar unit in the North African desert campaign, before being appointed an official artist with the service.

Paul Nash, Battle of Britain.

Nash's tumultuous painting of the Battle of Britain on a sunlit day in August 1940, with the swirling trails of the fighting planes, marks the first time for centuries that lethal single combat had been seen in island Britain. Day after day, people all over the south of England could look up to the skies, see the Spitfires take on the German Messerschmitts and follow the careering, uncontrolled trajectories of fatally wounded planes as they fell to earth.

Nash, who had painted the first World War of the twentieth century, and had lived to paint the Second, said, 'Even close behind the trenches in France, I never experienced the intensity of seeing those men and their planes taking each other on in the open sky.' He produced a superb series of paintings which capture the emotions of the earthbound observer. Of this picture, he wrote:

The painting is an attempt to give the sense of an aerial battle over a wide area and thus summarizes England's great aerial victory over Germany. After a hot, brilliant day, trails of aeroplanes, smoke tracks of dead or damaged machines falling, floating clouds, parachutes, balloons, the distant shores of the Continent, and new threatening formations of the Luftwaffe.

The British fighter pilots recalled viewing the landscape Nash portrays with great sentiment. 'Each day seemed full of blinding light and colour', said Johnny Johnson. As he patrolled over the Channel coast he saw:

The flat lands of Kent, the chequered fields and chalk downs of Sussex gapped by tiny rivers, and, on the far horizon the rolling country of Hampshire and Dorset. I was too high to pick out the hamlets and villages crouching under down and wold. Coming down, with the white cliffs at Beachy Head disentangling themselves from the haze. A few seconds later, I could recognize my airfield lying at the foot of the downs and fitting into the landscape as easily as a thrush on her nest.

The Luftwaffe fighter squadrons were now only thirty miles from Dover. Pondering other threats of invasion in England's history, Johnson and his comrades knew that all would be won or lost in the air. Yet, after a patrol over the Channel, they would land to be greeted by friends and girlfriends, take themselves off to the local pub or the bar, and discuss cricket and sports results. Johnson wryly recalled, at the height of the Battle of Britain, being soundly ticked off for 'talking shop' over a beer in the mess bar.

The accounts by British fighter pilots of the reality of combat in these skies reflect not only the danger but also the romance they clearly felt as knights of the sky. One of them, Tim Elkington, buoyed by his first victory in the Battle of Britain on 12 August 1940, painted a picture on his Hurricane fighter for good luck. His triumph in combat had come within a month of his being commissioned into RAF No 1 Squadron as a pilot officer, and only days after he had first flown a Hurricane at all. He had seen his first kill, a Messerschmitt Bf 109, plunge smoking to its end, down through the clouds over Harwich. His happy 'nose art', completed on 15 August, was a bright yellow figure called 'Eugene the Jeep', from the Popeye cartoons, a character supposed to have powers to see into the future. Nineteen-year-old Elkington's luck would take an unexpected turn just 24 hours later, when he was involved in one of the most widely remembered grand encounters between British and German fighters, played out in front of a watching civilian population all along the coast by the Solent. He would live to tell the tale, but only just.

Among the mesmerized onlookers was Elkington's half-American mother, Isabel, observing the many dogfights from her balcony on Hayling Island through her new husband's naval binoculars. She and Elkington's father, Alan, an Army major, had divorced when the boy was fourteen, and Elkington, an only child, had taken to the RAF joyfully. On this day, the young man had the job of 'top weaver', flying to and fro above his mates in No. 1 squadron to provide early warning of approaching enemy. Their flight leader that day was Sergeant Pilot Fred Berry, at the ripe old age of twenty-six a father figure with many years' flying experience.

The German raid was to prove the worst Tangmere had suffered, with buildings destroyed and twenty ground staff and civilians killed. The RAF that day would lose eight pilots, gain a Victoria Cross and log several spectacular crashes and rescues. Elkington's mother trained her binoculars on a lone Hurricane pursued by three German Bf 109s. It was a lovely sunny afternoon. She knew about the 'nose art', and recognized the plane as her boy's. Then his Hurricane took a hit – cannon fire from one of the Bf 109s chasing his tail.

It was later established that the Bf 109 was being flown by the Luftwaffe ace Major Helmut Wick, so Elkington, his eighteenth victim, was later to recall, 'He was quite an experienced chap, so I'm not too put out!' Wick's burst caused Elkington's fuel tank, positioned in the wing, to explode and erupt into flame, and it took the injured Elkington two attempts to bale out. Having slid back his cockpit canopy, and slipped his safety harness, he forgot to disconnect his radio and oxygen lines. 'No pain, just blood', he recalled, and the fine view he had of Portsmouth 'through the haze' was the last thing he saw before losing consciousness.

Elkington had not had time to inflate his 'Mae West' lifejacket, and as he drifted down 10,000ft in his parachute, the flight leader, Berry, knowing that the teenager would certainly drown without help, performed the brilliant flying feat of using his aircraft's slipstream to pull Elkington over the shore and on to the beach at West Wittering. The young man would thereafter think of Berry as his guardian angel.

Elkington's mother, on receiving a telephone call, set off to visit him in hospital in Chichester within the hour. His back was peppered with fragments of shrapnel, and a freckle-faced ambulance girl cut his trousers away to attend to wounds on his legs from the impact of a German cannon shell.

'A strange homecoming', he recalled, but he recovered well enough to rejoin the squadron on 1 October and scored two

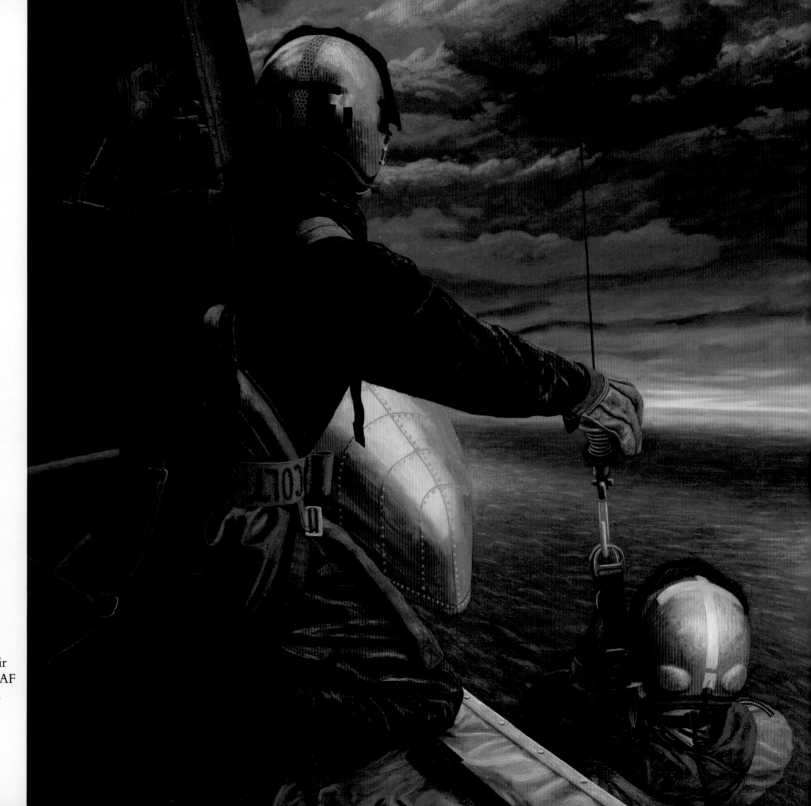

Geoffrey Staden, Air
Sea Rescue from RAF
Coltishall, Norfolk.

more credits that month: a 'probable' Junkers Ju 88 and the shared destruction of a Dornier.

Tim Elkington's account of being saved by the draught from his flight leader's plane highlights one of the lethal problems thrown up by the location of the Battle of Britain – much of it was fought over the English Channel.

Even though it was summer, and largely fine weather, pilots who baled out and ended in the water had only a one in five chance of being rescued. More than two hundred pilots and crew were lost in the Channel during those months. At a time when aircrew were desperately needed, such attrition was disastrous, and the air command summoned a number of meetings which resulted in the setting up of what became the Air Sea Rescue Service.

Geoffrey Staden's 1981 painting of a helicopter rescue shows how far the service has now come. Indeed, members of the Royal Family have served in its aircrew. But it began in 1940 with small motor boats and old planes – even biplanes – quartering the sea, directing the rescue boats and dropping little inflatable dinghies and protective clothing. Amphibious planes, the Sea Otter and the Walrus, were able, in reasonably calm conditions, to put down on the water and pick up survivors. By the end of the war, the service had more than a thousand vessels, including some 300 high-speed launches.

It was only in the 1960s that helicopters began to take over, and by 2020 there were ten locations around the UK coast fulfilling the inevitably ongoing task of saving aviators and others who found themselves in the sea.

Spitfire Handbook

The Spitfire pilot was presented by the Air Ministry with a daunting array of handbooks about his plane. Many of these contained minutely detailed diagrams of all the seventy-seven different instruments in his cockpit and the proper documentary format for reporting everything from a lost glove to the destruction of an enemy aircraft or the precise damage his Spitfire had suffered. How to roll, flick, dive, loop and carry out every sort of aerobatic manoeuvre was also described.

But one of the instruction manuals also contained plenty of terse and graphic instructions on how to fight in the air, beginning with the golden rule of silence:

> Never forget that the HUN is listening to nearly everything you say on the RT or in the 'local' pub. Be careful what you say on the former, and resist the temptation of describing even your most successful patrol at the latter. It would be very hard to do so without telling Hitler something that he would like to know.

Then there was the actual fighting in the air. Much of it followed the experience that had been gained in the First World War and set down in the *Diktat Boelcke*, for example about using the sun to hide an attack. But the homilies in the Spitfire handbook were quite clear:

> Never stop looking round. Out of every five minutes on patrol, four should be spent looking over your shoulder. Many pilots never saw the enemy fighter that got them.

Paul Nash, Totes Meer.

Always keep above your leader. It will help you to come into formation quickly. The man who is late lets the team down – sometimes right down. Take it for granted there is a Hun behind you. There often is!

The advantage of height is half the battle.

Always stick together for as long as possible. You can help each other in dogfights.

Use a head on attack against a formation if possible

A barrelled aileron turn is very effective with fighters. An increasing rate of turn prevents the enemy getting his sights on you and will usually give you a shot at him. Try and face an enemy fighter who is above you. Climb into the sun.

When out of ammunition don't hang about. Dive steeply with rocking turns to right and left.

If an enemy's bullets are getting uncomfortably close, do a quick barrel half roll and then rudder into a steep dive with aileron turns.

If all this failed, the Handbook then gave firm instructions on how to bale out:

First, lift your seat to the full-up position, slide back your hood and lock it fully open.

Undo your harness, take hold of the parachute rip cord, and then either stand up on the seat, or roll onto your back. Our old friends gravity and centrifugal force will have done the rest before you know they have started. If the aircraft is spinning, get out on the inside of the spin. If your clothes are soaked in petrol, switch off the engine and leave the throttle open, otherwise the sparks from the exhaust may act like the flint in your cigarette lighter.

Keep hold of your rip cord as you leave the aircraft. There is no need to pull it for the time being. Pilots who have pulled the rip cord immediately after getting out of the aircraft have been badly injured. The 109 will also find you harder to hit with the umbrella shut rather than open. You only fall 1,000 feet in 5 seconds. So there is really plenty of time.

Your gloves are most important if the plane has caught fire. If your right hand were to get burnt, you would not be able to feel for the rip cord.

The Handbook then went on to deal with damaged planes:

If your aircraft has been hit, test the hydraulic system at a safe height. If it has broken you can nearly always get the wheels down by diving and pulling out quickly, or rocking the aircraft with your rudder.

If your wing surface has been damaged, remember that the wing surface will stall first when holding off to land.

If you have been wounded and think you might pass out, turn the oxygen full on – it will help you a lot.

Then there is a whole section of 'Don'ts':

Don't forget to turn the firing button on.
Don't forget your radiator. Your guns need keeping warm.

Don't forget your oxygen at night. You need more. And
  don't wind your oxygen tube around your neck. It may
  choke you if you have to bale out.
Don't land with your wheels up after an exciting and
  successful combat. Some have.

After his evening's reading, the Spitfire pilot must indeed
have felt he was entitled to his visit to the 'local.'

The Pilots

Many of the Spitfire and Hurricane pilots recorded their
experiences. This is Geoffrey Page:

I was lucky because I had the unique experience of being
one of the very few pilots during the Battle of Britain
who had flown both the Hurricane and the Spitfire.
They were both lovable, but in their different ways – they
were delightful airplanes. I tend to give an example of
the bulldog and the greyhound, the Hurricane being the
bulldog and the greyhound being the Spitfire. One's a
sort of tough working animal and the other one's a sleek,
fast dog. But I think their characteristics were comparable
to the dog world. If anything, the Hurricane was slightly
easier. It wasn't as fast and didn't have the rate of climb.
But during the actual Battle of Britain itself, what
really evolved was that the Hurricanes would attack the
German bomber formations and the Spitfires, because of
their extra capability of climbing, they would go up and
attack the German fighter escorts. But in the earlier stages
I found that we were getting involved with both bombers
and fighters when we were flying Hurricanes.

Roland Beamont described one such encounter, escaping a
first attack by a group of German fighters:

I could see the rest of their formation still up above. I
thought, 'Right, I'll climb back up and see if I can pick
up a straggler.' But before I did that, a target presented
itself because right down across my front came a single
109. I rolled in after this Messerschmitt, half thinking
for a moment that it might be a Spitfire because it was so
unusual to see a single Messerschmitt by itself. Whether
he'd been hit or not, I don't know: he wasn't showing
any smoke, he was travelling fairly fast just diving towards
the sea as if he was getting the hell out of it and going
home, which is probably just what he was doing. Anyway,
I got on to his tail, fired a long burst. He slowed up and
then he rolled very violently up to the right. As he came
out of his roll I was back on his tail close in for another
burst, when I could see that his undercarriage was coming
down. He was also streaming grey smoke, might have
been coolant. We were down to about 1,200 feet then
over the fields of Dorset, the Purbeck Hills. He started
to side-slip fairly violently. He did another roll this time
with his wheels down and then did a diving, dirt turn
down towards the ground. I thought either he's going to
go in or he's actually aiming at a forced landing. I held

Richard Eurich, Dogfight over Portland.

off and he went round a field, lost speed, side-slipped quite sharply and he was obviously a very capable pilot. Eventually he went in to land on this field.

George Unwin described another:

I was at about 20,000 feet and I suddenly saw this lone Dornier, how he was on his own I'll never know, but he was off home. So I went after him. Now the drill against the Dornier was that he had a dustbin rear gunner, a dustbin hanging down below the fuselage, and you had to fix him first and then close in for the aircraft. This I did cleverly of course, I could see him shooting at me and I closed in and gave him a burst and shut him up, at least I thought I had. I never know to this day whether I did or I didn't or whether someone took his place, because as I closed right in on him and started shooting, I suddenly saw his rear gunner shooting back at me with little red sparks – you can see. I didn't pay much attention to it, I just thought he would stop another one and carried on firing for quite a while, quite a long burst, when suddenly I was covered in smoke. To my horror a hole appeared, I was leaning forward of course, as one did, to the gun-sight, and a hole appeared in this thing in front of my face. I thought, 'Good God, I must be dead or something, no blood, no nothing but I'm covered in smoke.' I thought I was on fire. So I whipped the hood back, undid my straps and started to get out. By this time I'd broken away and was going downhill. And I was halfway out of the cockpit,

when I suddenly saw that smoke was coming from the top of the engine, through the engine cowling, which is where the glycol pipe is, the coolant pipe; it was a really browny colour, it wasn't black smoke and I could smell it too, it was glycol. So I got back in and strapped myself in again, left the hood open and still went rapidly downhill in case somebody was following me and then started looking for a field and I found a field to land in. I waited until I'd found my field and got down to about 1,000 feet, dropped the undercarriage and did a forced landing in this field no trouble at all. I hadn't even got out of the cockpit before an Army jeep with a young subaltern and two soldiers with fixed bayonets came roaring through the gate and as soon as they saw it was one of ours they changed their attitude. I got a screwdriver from one of the soldiers and we took the top off and there it was; a bullet had gone through the glycol pipe, the top – the header – there was glycol all over the place.

This was Douglas Grice's experience:

I was flying by myself a thousand or a couple of thousand feet higher than the rest of the squadron and slightly behind, weaving like mad, looking right, left, centre, up, down, mostly back. When suddenly, out of the corner of my eye, I saw a flash over my left wrist and the next moment of course the cockpit was full of flames. The heat was enormous and I'd done two things absolutely instinctively. My left hand had gone to the handle of the

Elisabeth Frink, Eagle Squadron Memorial.

I was doing a left hand turn and my aircraft had gone on turning over on its back and I'd just fallen out! Anyway, there I was falling away and I did actually remember my parachute drill which was of course to wait before pulling the rip cord for two or three seconds. And I pulled it and there was a jerk and there I was floating down with a marvellous canopy and about a couple of miles inland. I could look down and see the land, so I thought at least I won't be going into the sea. Something seemed to have happened to my face – there were bits of skin flapping around my eyes! And my mouth felt very uncomfortable. Of course, I'd been burnt. Well, very shortly after that, I was over the coast and a few minutes later I was a mile out to sea, and a few minutes after that I was two miles out to sea. Well the sea gradually approached and I wasn't a bit worried because I was coming down, going to splash down, only a couple of hundred yards from a little fishing trawler. Well the splash happened and I got rid of my harness and looked round and there was the trawler and I waved like mad and it eventually arrived and they hauled me on board.

hood, my right hand had gone to the pin of my harness and I was pulling with both hands and the next moment I was out in the open air. I'd made no attempt to jump out of that aircraft and of course I was straining back from the flames and the heat. And what I think had happened was,

Elisabeth Frink's eagle, soaring above Grosvenor Square in London, recognizes the 244 Americans who came over to join the Eagle Squadrons in Britain in the two years before the United States actually entered the Second World War. Seventy-one of them were killed.

They were funded and organized by Charles Sweeny, an American businessman in London who had himself come over to join the French Foreign Legion and then the Lafayette Air Squadron in France in the First World War. At the outbreak of the Second War he gathered together some American veterans of Lafayette days, as well as some young recruits, to put together, in France, a successor to the Great War squadron. But the fall of France meant he had to move them to England, where his initiative was welcomed by the Royal Air Force.

By the summer of 1941 there were three Eagle fighter squadrons flying Spitfires and Hurricanes, The next year, after Pearl Harbor, the squadrons and their support teams were transferred to the United States Army Air Force Fighter Command.

Strategy

The Battle of Britain, turning point of the war though it was, had been a clear-cut defensive contest – stop the bombers and the fighters getting through to the cities and airfields of Britain. But since the early days of military flying in the First World War there had been extraordinarily little attention paid to the strategy of war in the air.

The schoolboys of England had been brought up on how Drake used his whole fleet to take on the Armada, rather than allowing each ship to fight separately; and Nelson had famously devised and carried out fleet orders to carve through the French battle line at Trafalgar. But with the exception of a few notable individuals, little thought had gone into how aircraft, particularly bombers, should be used in war. What should the strategy be?

Towards the end of the Second World War, *The Times* correspondent Arthur Narracott, wrote:

In the early stages of the war, before we understood the use of air power as well as we do now, one of the most common misuses of our air forces was to send out aircraft in 'penny packets' to help any small section of ground troops who temporarily found themselves in difficulty either from enemy dive bombers, or some other hostile aircraft, from enemy tanks, artillery or even machine guns which were proving a nuisance. This was a flagrant misuse of the air … [although] a sub-lieutenant in the field, whose company of men is being attacked by two or three enemy bombers, quite naturally feels that he deserves one or two RAF fighters to drive off the enemy machines.

Narracott, who had himself seen action at Dunkirk and had later flown in Lancaster bombers, became an apostle to men like the Italian General Douhet, the American pilot Billy Mitchell and British leaders Tedder and Trenchard, who had fought to establish that the use of air power in war should be decided at the very highest level. The key criteria, as Air Chief Marshal Tedder was to express them, were: concentration, flexibility and mobility of force.

The power of concentration of a bomber force emerged in the wake of the German attacks on Britain in the spring of 1941. In one attack on London in April, some 350 aircraft dropped about 500 tons of bombs. But the RAF were already beginning to put into service heavier bombers, which would within little more than a year be capable of delivering ten

Julius Stafford Baker, Lancaster in the Desert.

times that weight of bombs in half an hour. This soon led to the thousand-bomber raids which caused such devastation to cities and factories in the Ruhr and beyond. The British, under Air Marshal 'Bomber' Harris, and joined in 1942 by the American Eighth and Ninth Air Forces, and later their Liberators and Flying Fortresses, were able to cause tremendous havoc to the production capacity of the German war effort.

A key part of the success of bombing efforts was the development of a strategy which included formation flying with fighter protection, pathfinder planes dropping marker flares on targets, and the positioning of fighter escorts above the bombers. By 1943, the bombers were able to reach Berlin and establish a pattern of carpet-bombing, with more than 2,000 tons of bombs being dropped on successive nights. The strategy was, from the first leaflet raids on Berlin, to attack civilian morale, and then also to disrupt and destroy the supply of German armaments.

But the air power theorists were also determined to show how a combined approach with the Army and Navy could also produce results. In North Africa, when Rommel's 2,000-mile push had been halted to the west of Egypt, Montgomery, the Eighth Army commander, and Air Marshal Coningham, in charge of the Desert Air Force, jointly planned the assault which was to start at El Alamein and remove the Germans and the Italians from the field all along the southern Mediterranean coast. The story goes that they ate every meal together, and had their two personal caravans placed just yards away from each other. Certainly, as the Army moved forward, the RAF and their planes and equipment moved with them, operating often from only ten miles or so behind the advancing troops.

Fighting the V1s and V2s

Leslie Cole's picture of fighters attacking flying bombs, the V1s, might raise eyebrows today. The analogy might be Tornadoes taking on NASA space rockets.

But the reaction of British defences to the arrival of the V1 attacks was remarkably effective. Known to Londoners as 'doodlebugs' or 'buzz bombs', the unmanned V1s travelled at 340 mph – faster than a Spitfire, although the Spitfires, in a dive from above, could reach them. However the V1s had limited range, and it was only after D-Day in 1944 that the attacks on London began, from launch pads along the Channel coast. The Royal Observer Corps rapidly established a radar and radio screen along the south coast which proved to give accurate and sufficient warning to the RAF. The V1s were actually very difficult to shoot down, and cannon fire often had little apparent effect on them. But some RAF pilots developed an extraordinarily daring and difficult manoeuvre, in which they brought the wing of their own plane just underneath the wing of the flying bomb – sometimes a matter of inches away – thus disrupting the airflow around it sufficiently to change its course. The number of V1s that fell in the sea or the countryside was genuinely attributed to this courageous tactic, and by August 1944 the Spitfires and Mosquitoes were accounting for 80 per cent of the attacking bombs.

Leslie Cole. Flying Bomb.

Paul Nash, The Battle of Germany.

It was a different matter when the V2s appeared in September 1944. As the German engineer Dornberger boasted, they were the first true spacecraft, reaching a height of 50 miles above the earth before hurtling down on their targets. The RAF could offer no defence against them, and its only option was to attack the rockets' launch stations. As the Allies progressed across France and into Germany, the V2 sites became ever more vulnerable, and the last rocket to hit England landed in Orpington, Kent in March 1945.

Their technology was to live on, however, and flourish, into the space age.

Bombing

In the Second World War bombing became much the commonest experience of the conflict for most of the citizens of Europe.

Paul Nash's 1944 painting executed, despite his advancing years, in his most modernist style, aimed to encompass the totality of this aspect of war from the air. He wrote a detailed note about the painting:

The moment of the picture is when the city, lying under the uncertain light of the moon, awaits the blow at its heart. In the background a gigantic column of smoke arises from the recent destruction of an outlying factory which is still fiercely burning. These two objects – pillar and moon – seem to threaten the city no less than the flights of bombers even now towering in the red sky.

In contrast to the suspense of the waiting city under the quiet though baleful moon, the other half of the picture shows the opening of the bombardment. The entire area of sky and background and part of the middle distance are violently agitated. Here colours are used to suggest explosion and detonation. In the foreground the floating discs may be part of a flight of paratroops or the crews of aircraft forced to bale out.

The unique and dazzling stained glass window in the Royal Air Force club in London was created by the Yorkshire artist Helen Whittaker, who works at Barley Studio in Dunnington. The window was installed in 2016, more than seventy years after the last Lancaster bomber returned from the final raid on Berlin. Like the installation of the Bomber Command memorial in Hyde Park in 2012, this long delay reflects, perhaps, the moral ambiguity haunting those who rained bombs from the skies and razed whole cities in fire and storm.

There seems little doubt now that the thousand-bomber raids and the destruction of Cologne, Hamburg and Dresden, did indeed diminish the capacity, if not the morale, of the enemy. But the inevitable obliteration of huge numbers of the old, of children, of women – maybe 25,000 in Dresden alone – cast a long shadow over the sacrifices of the Allied bomber

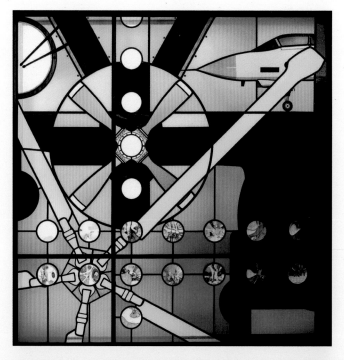

Helen Whittaker, RAF Club Stained Glass Window.

Bomber Command
Memorial, Hyde Park.

crews, before the assessment of historians finally gave it a justifiable perspective.

Even today, Air Forces and their crews feel the need to justify the bombing tactics used in contemporary conflicts. Indeed, the Royal Air Force Museum in London contains a section in which pilots affirm that the bombing of Libya in 2011, for example, was undertaken to free the Libyan people from the dictatorship of Colonel Gaddafi – collateral damage though there undoubtedly was.

These memorials finally arrived only after long and determined campaigns by survivors to recognize the bravery and sacrifice of the three quarters of their Bomber Command comrades who did not live to see the coming of victory.

Leonard Cheshire

In 1943, Leonard Cheshire – later to be awarded the Victoria Cross – wrote an extraordinary book, *Bomber Pilot*.

He had already flown a hundred missions in Whitley and Halifax bombers, and he describes in great detail attacking Cologne, Berlin, the Ruhr. Many – indeed, most – of his fellow pilots, friends and colleagues, including his brother Christopher, had been lost. But alongside the emotional stories of near-misses and determined raids through intense anti-aircraft fire and enemy fighters, Cheshire displays a professional approach, almost a detachment, which seems beyond credibility in the circumstances.

He describes returning to flying after a break, during which he was sent on a public relations trip to the United States and Canada, and having his first encounter with the new German defences:

The guns, it is true, were much the same as ever, a little more powerful and a little more accurate, but where there used to be one, there were now two, three, four, and in places even ten.

As for the searchlights, the change was remarkable. Once they had been ineffective at 8,000 feet, now they were effective at 18,000. Where before there were fifty or sixty, there were now two or three hundred. Where once we had gambolled around in utter freedom, there was a festering bed, from Denmark down to Abbeville, of thousands.

Yes, night bombing was very different from what it had been eighteen months ago, night fighters and a continuous barrier of shells and searchlights, and, more aggravating still, a host of knobs and technical instruments which we would have scorned in summer 1940.

In spite of all this, the trips were no more interesting than before, nor were they any more exciting. The work was no longer a novelty. More technical skill was required. So the first carefree exultant joy was gone. In its place appeared an atmosphere of quiet enjoyment.

Cheshire was to sail, even saunter, through all the lethal developments of the air war, and survived to be an airborne witness of the atomic bombs on Japan. He and his wife then, of course, became the founders of the Cheshire Homes for

Wilhelm Rudolph, Dresden.

the disabled which are to this day one of the great pillars of the post-war caring society.

It was sixty-seven years after the end of the war before Liam O'Connor's memorial to the 55,000 men killed in the service of Bomber Command was finally unveiled by the Queen, in her Diamond Jubilee year, at Hyde Park Corner in London. The stone structure contains a bronze group by Philip Jackson of seven aircrew who have just emerged from their bomber. It is built to reflect the way a Wellington bomber appeared. The metal used came from the wreckage of a Halifax bomber found in Belgium in 1997 and retrieved by the Canadian government. More than 10,000 of the Bomber Command crew who died were Canadians.

On three days in the early summer of 1942, as the residents of Wetherby in Yorkshire later recalled, the bright night sky was literally darkened by aircraft.

These were Halifax bombers – and to see one now is to be reminded quite what massive creatures they were – more than a hundred of them from the half dozen airfields in that part of Yorkshire, gathering to join the thousand-bomber raids being launched on German cities. Their first target was to be Cologne.

By the time the attackers crossed the sea, they numbered 1,047 aircraft, of which more than 1,000 were to safely return. They formed a dense stream which, flying at 13,000 feet, unloaded all its bombs on the city in only ninety minutes just after midnight. More than two thousand fires were started, and more than 20,000 houses were damaged or destroyed, as well as more than 10,000 factories and commercial buildings. Old Cologne was almost completely obliterated by this new technique of aerial destruction which was to culminate three years later in the ultimate firestorm, consuming Dresden and 20,000 or more of its inhabitants and refugees.

Wilhelm Rudolph's woodcuts of the Dresden destruction, which he lived through – and which burned much of his prewar work – are the most eloquent testimony to the worst that man could wreak from the skies, until the ultimate apocalypse of Hiroshima and Nagasaki.

Eric Ravilious

Eric Ravilious was perhaps the most intrepid of all the Second World War artists. Indeed, he was to die when flying from Iceland on a search and rescue mission for a missing RAF plane.

Ravilious's picture of the aircraft carrier HMS *Glorious*, with Hurricanes, Gloster Gladiators and Swordfish buzzing like hornets around her, was painted less than twenty-four hours before the ship was to meet her doom. The artist was aboard her accompanying cruiser HMS *Highlander* in the confused and failing scramble to save Norway from German occupation in the spring of 1940.

A squadron leader from the carrier *Ark Royal*, John Ievers, was sent to the makeshift Norwegian airfield where the remaining RAF planes were based, with the only option being to get them out on *Glorious*. He later said:

I spent the last few days with the squadrons, and although my knowledge of deck-landing in Hurricanes was nil, I was able to give them some rudimentary rules to follow.

Eric Ravilious, HMS *Glorious*.

On the day, we *Ark Royal* pilots followed the Hurricanes out to *Glorious* and circled round while they landed on, with the only damage being one broken tail wheel, which was a remarkable feat of skill on the part of the squadron pilots. I then landed on myself and was awaiting instructions for being struck down below when a chap came down from flyco and said, 'Sorry. There's no room for you. You'll have to go on to *Ark Royal*.' I objected strongly, because I wanted to stay with the squadron. But I was overruled.

Glorious was to be struck the very next day by a shell from the German battleship *Scharnhorst* sixteen miles away over the horizon. Her flight deck and lift were disabled and she soon went down. Radio silence meant that no serious attempt was made to rescue the sailors and aircrew on board, and all but forty perished. Ievers said, 'I suspect I was the last person to land on and fly off from her deck. A lucky escape.'

Glorious had been a monument to the successes and the failures of the Royal Navy's adoption of air power. Unlike the lamentably slow recognition of the potential menace of the submarine, the Navy had quickly recognized that the aeroplane could provide reconnaissance and protection to the fleet in a new and unique way. *Glorious* was built in 1916, and by 1918 she had her two gun turrets adapted to carry an aircraft – the Sopwith Camel. These remarkable planes were able to get up enough engine speed from these so-called flight platforms to be catapulted into the air and away.

In many ways, the operation of fighting planes at sea, right up to the arrival of vertical take-off, seems in retrospect extraordinarily crude. Even in the 1960s, carriers like HMS *Albion* had to turn into what wind they could find, attach their planes by a wire rope to a grown-up version of a child's catapult and then hurl them over the bow. Catching them on the way back was simply a matter of the pilot dangling a hook under the tail and hoping he could drop his machine just at the right spot to catch the wire ropes stretched across the flight deck. If not, he just had to go round and try again.

Glorious had been built in the First World War as a cruiser, but was converted into an aircraft carrier in the 1920s. She was selected for conversion because she was big enough to create a flight deck sufficiently long to allow planes to rev up and take off as though they were on a terrestrial airfield. The early planes were equipped with floats, so that they could come down on the sea and then be craned back on board.

By the outbreak of the Second World War, *Glorious* had been equipped with aircraft and was serving in the Mediterranean. But flying on and off her was still a somewhat hand-to-mouth affair. In the Norway campaign she was required to carry and dispatch Spitfires and Hurricanes destined to be delivered to and operated from Norwegian airfields. But there was still an assumption that they might have to be landed back on board. With commendable initiative, one pilot discovered that a sackful of sand carried under the tail of his plane was enough to slow it down on landing and diminish the risk of tipping over the end of the deck..

Throughout his time as a war artist, Ravilious made the greatest effort to grasp the realities of war in the air. In

Scotland he managed to get himself airborne in the Walrus seaplanes based at RAF Dundee. When he was later moved south he started flying in the rear cockpit of the Tiger Moths based at Sawbridgeworth in Hertfordshire, always carrying his sketch book. When he was lost on the search and rescue patrol in Iceland, no trace was ever found of him or his plane.

Flying Fortresses

The medieval aura surrounding the early fighting in the sky – jousting, fencing, single combat – scarcely dimmed through the two world wars. The Flying Fortresses of the US Air Force really were castles in the air.

Although fighter protection for attacking bombers remained essential, the bomber crews themselves were equipped with the most advanced defensive weapons. The Flying Fortresses were Boeing bombers given their nickname by an astonished newspaper reporter who saw the new models in Seattle bristling with machine guns – thirteen of them in the later models. Indeed, they became known to the Luftwaffe as 'flying porcupines'.

But the ancient principle of a strong defensive wall was not forgotten. One USAF Fortress pilot, Wally Hoffman, said, 'The plane can be cut and slashed almost to pieces by enemy fire and still bring its crew home.' One Fortress even survived a midair collision with a Focke Wulf and still got its crew back unscathed.

The Germans found they had to fire hundreds of cannon shots to bring a Fortress down, and the only effective way was to attack directly from the front, where the pilot had no protective armour. But this was a hazardous practice, since the Fortress's front gunner was ensconced in its distinctive glass nose cone.

The Fortresses, however, were not immune to other fates. A formation of them actually flew into Pearl Harbor as the Japanese were attacking; and then, as the Americans dithered on Formosa, almost all were destroyed on the ground.

But in Europe, and later in the Pacific, the Fortresses were a huge, maybe even a decisive, factor. The Japanese Zero fighters could not really reach the height at which the bombers operated, and the Fortresses sank enough enemy shipping to make a crucial contribution to victory in the Battle of the Bismarck Sea. In Europe they became the main daylight raiders, crippling large parts of the German aircraft industry.

Nicolas Trudgian's painting records a legendary incident when a Fortress, badly damaged, was actually escorted back to the safety of the Allied lines by a Messerschmitt pilot who had seen that the crew were wounded. The tale was told in 1945, but it was only forty-five years later that the remaining American crew managed to trace the identity of the German pilot, Franz Stigler, and get to meet him and thank him for their lives.

The Fortresses were at the centre of the colossal programme of American aircraft construction in the Second World War. By 1944 there were more than 80,000 American military planes in service based at more than 1,000 airfields across the world. But in the course of the war more than 60,000 aircraft were lost.

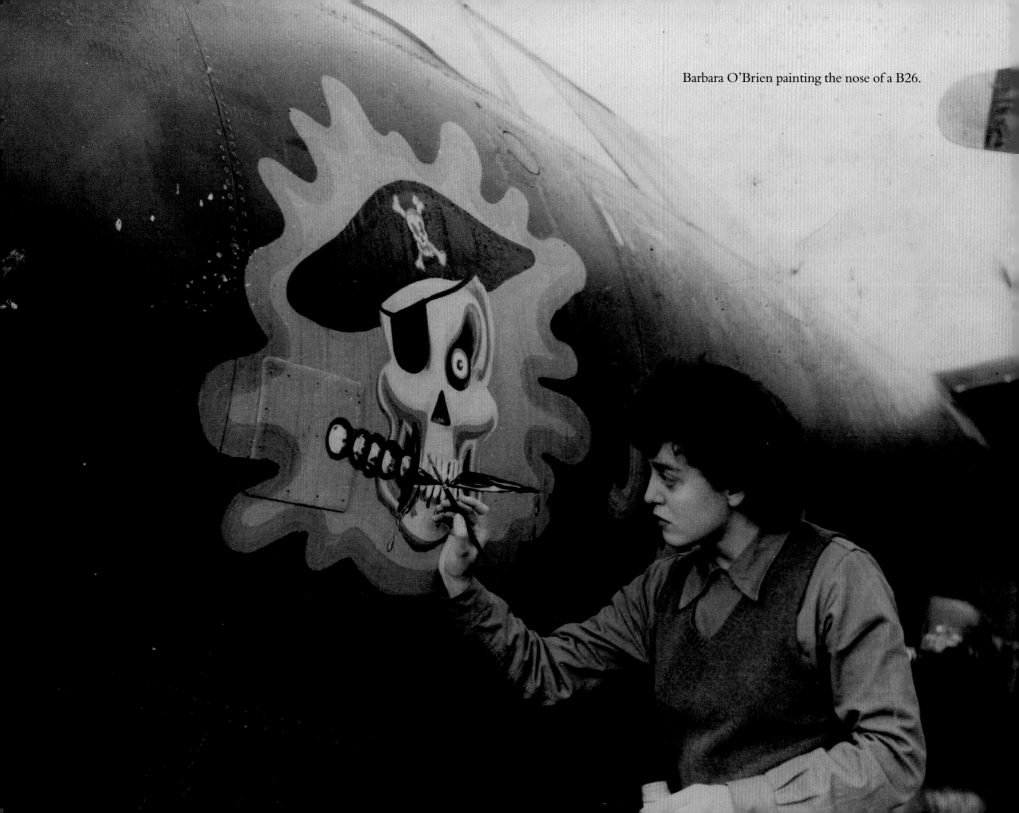

Barbara O'Brien painting the nose of a B26.

Nicolas Trudgian, Flying Fortress.

Air Gunners

Charles Cundall's painting of an air gunner is a rare tribute by an artist to the men who manned the guns in the bombers.

In contrast to the dashing, vertiginous visions of the pilots hurling their craft around the skies, the gunners were cramped, lonely figures, enduring often freezing cold isolation for eight hours or more on the raids over Germany, until an enemy fighter suddenly appeared and they were called on to try and strike it down.

This was the other side of fighting in the sky, more like machine guns and rifles in the trenches than the glamour of the pilots and the fighter planes. Yet the gunners' work was just as crucial to the war effort, and the risks were as daunting. Nearly half of all the Royal Air Force gunners were killed in the war. In the difficult days of 1943, an air gunner was lucky to last more than half a dozen missions, but the gunners and their machine guns were fundamental to the ability of the bombers to get through to their targets.

The Fortress had a gun turret in the nose and the tail, as well as turrets above the cockpit. Unprepared as the British and Americans had been for many aspects of the war, they had developed one crucial device – the rotating gun turret. The two Air Forces had understood that powered gun turrets could deliver enormously greater effectiveness than a gunner having to manhandle his weapon round to take aim and fire. As early as 1934, rotating turrets were being tried on the RAF's big Blackburn Perth bombers.

The Germans, over-confident perhaps in the wake of their bombers' performance in the Spanish Civil War, were very late in developing powered turrets for their bombers.

Cundall's painting shows how tight and intricate the turrets were – at the Yorkshire Air Museum in Elvington several surviving turrets still display how almost inhumanly cramped the air gunners were. Some planes carried up to 10,000 rounds of ammunition, fed in enormous chains directly through to the machine guns. But this was the equipment which allowed enough of the bombers to get through and wreak such utter destruction on German towns and war industries.

W. J. Lawrence, who served in Lancasters with No. 5 Group of RAF Bomber Command and wrote an account of their history, related one example of what his colleagues had to endure – in this case a raid on Düsseldorf. Flight Lieutenant William Reid was captain of a Lancaster from 61 Squadron.

Soon after he crossed the Dutch coast, his windscreen was suddenly smashed. A Messerschmitt 110 was attacking. The Lancaster's heating system had failed, and the rear gunner's hands had grown so cold that he could not hold his microphone to give warning of the enemy's approach. At first he was also unable to fire his guns, but then he managed to drive the Messerschmitt off. Flight Lieutenant Reid had been wounded in the head, shoulders and hands; the elevator trimming tabs were damaged; the rear turret was damaged; and the communications system and the compasses were out of action. But Reid decided to press on towards Düsseldorf.

Soon after, the Lancaster was attacked by a Focke Wulf 190 and the enemy's fire raked the whole length of the

Charles Cundall,
Air Gunner
Prepared for
Action.

bomber. With his turret already damaged and only one of his guns working, it was impossible for the rear gunner to aim accurately. The navigator was killed and the wireless operator so badly wounded that he later died. Reid was himself wounded again, and his flight engineer, himself wounded in the arm, gave him oxygen from the portable supply.

The captain was, however, determined to carry on. He had memorized his course into the target and he flew on so steadily that his bomb aimer, cut off in his compartment by the failure of the communication system, had no idea that the captain was wounded, or that there had been other casualties.

The Lancaster reached Düsseldorf fifty minutes later. The bomb aimer released his bombs, and a photograph taken in the act of bombing showed that the aircraft was then flying right over the centre of the target. Reid set course for home, steering by the Pole Star and the moon. He grew weak from loss of blood and almost lost consciousness, but the flight engineer kept the Lancaster in the air. Once over England, when an airfield was sighted, Reid revived, resumed control and made ready to land, though blood was still affecting his vision. He made a safe landing, although one leg of the undercarriage collapsed.

Reid 'for his superb courage and leadership' was subsequently awarded the Victoria Cross.

The Blitz

Edward Burra called his painting 'Blue Baby Blitz', and it is suitably threatening, with the bombed-out people at the bottom, yet also distinctly derisive.

The Blitz on London began in the middle of September 1940 as the main phase of the Battle of Britain ended. Hitler, it seems, was hoping to destroy the morale of the British and induce them to seek peace. The British Government, with memories of Zeppelin raids on London only two decades earlier, was also concerned about the country's morale. Thousands of children were evacuated from the city to the countryside; there was an urgent programme of building air raid shelters; a complete night-time blackout was instituted; and the recruitment of a large corps of air raid wardens began.

The Blitz started with a massive daylight raid on 15 September, and this was followed by more than fifty consecutive day or night raids. By October, nearly 400 German bombers were appearing over London in a single raid. As the year turned, there were huge raids on other ports and cities. One day in April 1941, more than 700 bombers attacked Plymouth, and there was heavy damage to Liverpool, Hull, and Coventry.

But by May, the RAF's new Beaufighters were starting to exact a toll on the raiders, with more than thirty bombers shot down in one night. By May 1941, the Blitz had almost ended. British morale had not been broken and, in any case, Hitler had turned his attention to the invasion of Russia.

London's underground stations had provided the main shelter each night for nearly 200,000 citizens, with queues forming for an hour or more before they were admitted. In the end, for all the damage to homes and businesses, the death toll was about 20,000, significantly less than the Government's predictions; and large numbers of the evacuees returned to the city.

Edward Burra, Blue Baby Blitz.

Priscilla Thorneycroft, Night in an
Underground Shelter.

Arthur Burgess, Sunderland Flying Boat.

Edward Burra's contemptuous depiction of the Blue Baby was borne out by the widespread public disdain for the Luftwaffe's efforts.

Sunderlands

Arthur Burgess's picture of a Sunderland flying boat shows an aircraft around which many epic tales accumulated: at once a bomber, a reconnaissance plane, a U-boat hunter, an air sea rescuer, a Berlin Airlift stalwart after the war and a personnel carrier.

A Sunderland evacuated more than eighty soldiers at a time from in front of the advancing German troops in Crete in 1943. Another scooped up all thirty-four crew from a ship sunk in the North Sea just a month after the outbreak of war. The first U-boat kill by a Sunderland was in July 1940 in the North Atlantic. Eight years later, Sunderlands were flying dozens of sorties a day, taking off from a river, landing on a lake and carrying supplies into the beleaguered Western sectors of Berlin, after the Soviets cut off all surface links to the city in 1948.

During the war, Sunderlands took part in extraordinary air sea rescue efforts in the English Channel, the North Sea and the Atlantic approaches, saving more than 8,000 Allied aircrew, as well as more than 5,000 men from wrecked and torpedoed ships, not to mention more than a hundred Luftwaffe personnel.

But the plane was also a fearsome fighting machine. It carried not only bombs but up to sixteen machine guns in turrets all round the aircraft. One Sunderland, attacked by eight Junkers over the Bay of Biscay, succeeded in destroying three of them and crippling the others to such an extent that they had to break off the fight. Then, damaged though it was, it managed to make the 350 miles back to Cornwall, where the pilot succeeded in putting her down off Praa Sands. One of the crew had been mortally wounded, but the other ten made it through the surf to safety.

Sadly, in the malign fortunes of war, only a few weeks later, nine of them – all but the pilot, Colin Walker – were lost aboard another Sunderland.

Air Sea Rescue

From the lamentably inadequate air sea rescue operations at the beginning of the Second World War there eventually evolved a determined and sophisticated service. One bomber crew was rescued from the sea 700 miles north of Shetland. A number of crews survived for seven, eight or even nine days after their planes had come down in the Bay of Biscay and the North Atlantic.

In 1943, the crew of a Halifax bomber found themselves ditched almost within sight of the German-occupied Dutch coast. Two Typhoons and a Mustang spotted their dinghy, and a rescue mission was set in train, two Walrus seaplanes setting off from Kent with an escort of Spitfires and Typhoons.

Both Walruses put down and, between them, picked up six crew members from the dinghy. But the sea was so rough that the Walrus pilots could not take off and decided to taxi on the surface to put at least some distance between them and the enemy coast. Eventually, after half an hour, one of the Walrus pilots, with two of the six on board, felt he could attempt a take-off. He succeeded, despite a pair of German Focke Wulfs passing right over him. The other Walrus pilot continued taxiing, although his plane was proving difficult to control in the continuing heavy seas, with waves more than 10 feet high. After six hours the Walrus ran out of fuel. Then an Air Sea Rescue motorboat got to them and took the plane in tow. But after an hour the pilot asked the boat to take him, his crew and the rescued flyers on board, and the tow rope was cut. Somehow the Walrus eventually managed to beach itself on a shoal off the Essex coast. From there a Navy destroyer got another tow on board and delivered it back to Harwich, where it was repaired sufficiently to go back into service.

The whole operation had saved the six crew more or less from under the guns of the Germans and had involved, as well as the motorboat and the destroyer, at least eleven planes, Spitfires, Typhoons and Hurricanes, as well as the Walruses.

Bitter experience propelled a long series of improvements in methods of rescuing aircrew from the sea. When the Battle of Britain began, fighter pilots were equipped only with Mae West vests to help them survive in the water. But after more than 1,000 aircrew died in the waters of the Channel and the North Sea in the first eighteen months of the war, action became imperative.

First, there was the issue of location: where were the men needing rescue? The RAF even turned to the pigeon fanciers of Great Britain. Two pigeons, confined to a little box, were procured to join every possible flight, ready to be dispatched with a message from the downed plane crews. There is only one record of this avian service actually helping to achieve a rescue, and winning the animal VC, the Dicken Medal. Sadly, many birds perished in the unfriendly conditions over the sea.

Then little dinghies were attached to the Mae Wests which could be inflated by the wearer, and the rescue boats became faster and more seaworthy. Above all, the RAF realized it needed planes to look for lost aircrew. First, there were planes begged from the Navy and adapted to carry dinghies which could be dropped near the men in the water. Then it was realized that these required some means of propulsion – especially away from the occupied French coast – so paddles were included. Later, even little engines were dropped, and survival rations were upgraded from chocolate and Horlicks tablets to more scientifically developed nutrition.

Above all, however, the rescue services realized they needed to be able to put down planes on the water and pick the crews up directly, and the Walrus and the Sunderland came along to fill the bill. The crews of these aircraft had to assess and cope with the most daunting conditions. After one Sunderland came down in the Bay of Biscay, the twelve crew managed to get into two of the dinghies. They had survived more than three days, when another Sunderland found them. The conditions were so rough that the men in the dinghies tried to wave their rescuers away. But after jettisoning his depth charges, the pilot decided to risk putting down on the sea. On the third attempt he succeeded and taxied towards the dinghies. The men paddled towards the plane, were dragged on board, and the Sunderland managed just enough leeway to take off. The full crew were safely delivered back to their base in Pembroke Dock, after one of the most challenging of the service's rescue missions.

The Air Sea Rescue service were aware that the most important task of all was to educate crew in what to do once they or their plane landed in the water. Detailed guidelines were given in order to avoid the mistakes made by downed airmen which had contributed needlessly to the deaths of those who had survived such a crash. The guidelines recommended that there should be 56oz of water in the dinghy. No water on the first day, unless exhausted or wounded, went the instruction; after that, 14oz; then after five days, 2oz. Without water, it was stated, a man can survive only four to six days; sea water is useless.

This produced the first of the three golden rules for men in a dinghy: make arrangements to collect rainwater. Second, bale the dinghy. Third, fix the weather apron. Air crews were given pages of further instructions about not removing clothing, however wet, about how to try to sail a dinghy, and much other detailed guidance. But it was only after many men were lost at sea that full training seems to have been given to all air crew. And only with the arrival of the American air forces were effective radio and location systems made available.

Swordfish

Robert Taylor's painting of the Royal Navy's Swordfish planes attacking the Italian fleet at Taranto in November 1940 records one of the many successful episodes in the story of this unlikely looking twin-winged 'Stringbag' aircraft – a plane immensely less speedy and glamorous than its contemporaries, the Spitfire and the Hurricane. Yet more than 2,000 of them were built during the Second World War, most being put together in Yorkshire, with various parts manufactured in workshops around Leeds and then trundled through the city's suburbs to be assembled at nearby Sherburn in Elmet.

The Stringbag could barely exceed 140 mph, but its ability to fly effectively at very low level made it almost uniquely capable of delivering torpedoes and hunting U-boats.

The attack on Taranto came at a time when Rommel's Afrika Corps and the Italians were rolling across the western deserts of North Africa. Only the island of Malta – just 100 miles off the North African coast – offered the British Mediterranean forces a base from which the Axis supply lines could be attacked.

The Swordfish from Malta and British aircraft carriers had already executed a vital mission against the French navy, which had holed up in the Algerian port of Mers el Kebir after the collapse of France in May 1940. Twelve Swordfish from the carrier HMS *Eagle* had conducted a torpedo attack against the ships anchored at Mers, destroying a French battleship and damaging the majority of the remaining French ships, to such an extent that the Vichy French navy never became a serious adversary in the long war to ensure the safe passage of supplies through the Mediterranean to Montgomery and the Allied forces in Egypt.

The Taranto attack, by Swordfish from the aircraft carrier *Illustrious* against the Italian fleet in its base in south-east Italy, heavily damaged three battleships, plus cruisers and destroyers,

Robert Taylor, Swordfish.

Richard Eurich, Convoy Attack.

to such an extent that the Italian navy could subsequently make only sporadic sallies against Allied shipping. The Swordfish pilots' tactics, coming in low to avoid torpedo nets and using torpedoes especially adapted for shallow water, attracted such attention from the Japanese – already, it would seem, pondering the strategies they would use a year later at Pearl Harbor – that they dispatched a military team down from Rome to see how such destruction had been successfully contrived.

Five months later in the North Sea, it was Swordfish squadrons from the aircraft carriers *Victorious* and *Ark Royal* which managed to cripple and then destroy the German battleship *Bismarck*. Post-war theories suggested that it was the very slowness of the planes, trundling along at 140 mph scarcely above wave height, which allowed them to reach their target. For the battleship's very modern guns, designed to fire into the line of flight of an attacker, were shooting at thin air well ahead of the Swordfish. And the guns, too, it seems, could not be lowered enough to hit the planes. Suffice it to say, the *Bismarck* went down, and most of the Swordfish made it back to their carriers.

By the end of 1941, Swordfish were engaged in U-boat hunting, and one had been the first plane to find and destroy a U-boat at night, off Gibraltar. And two dozen Swordfish based in Malta were wreaking heavy damage on the Axis shipping carrying Rommel's supplies.

This ancient looking biplane was to survive on active service right through to the end of the Second World War, before its honourable retirement. There are still intact versions at the Fleet Air Arm's museum in Somerset.

Malta

Denis Barnham's picture of a dogfight over Malta in 1942 marks the end of a two-year-long ordeal, during which Britain's Mediterranean colony was subjected to the most prolonged period of aerial bombardment in the entire war. Malta is only about seventeen miles long by ten wide, and nearly a quarter of its population lived round the Royal Navy base at Grand Harbour – but as war loomed, the Navy had moved almost all its fleet away to Alexandria in Egypt. Malta's defences consisted of half a dozen ancient Gloster Gladiator biplanes.

In the two years after Italy joined Germany in declaring war, Malta was attacked by enemy bombers more than a thousand times. On the very first day in June 1940, nearly a hundred Italian planes bombed the island, including the main airfield at Luqa. The RAF managed to get three of the old Gladiators into the air, and though one was shot down, the remainder managed not only to survive but actually shoot down several Italian bombers.

At one point there were literally no serviceable aircraft available to the RAF in Malta. The planes that eventually did arrive – mainly Hurricanes – were outclassed by the German Messerschmitts, which began the next effort to take Malta out of the war with three or more air raids every day, destroying among other things an entire squadron of Wellington bombers that the RAF had managed to dispatch to the island.

Yet Malta held out – to be eventually honoured with the award of the George Cross for outstanding communal

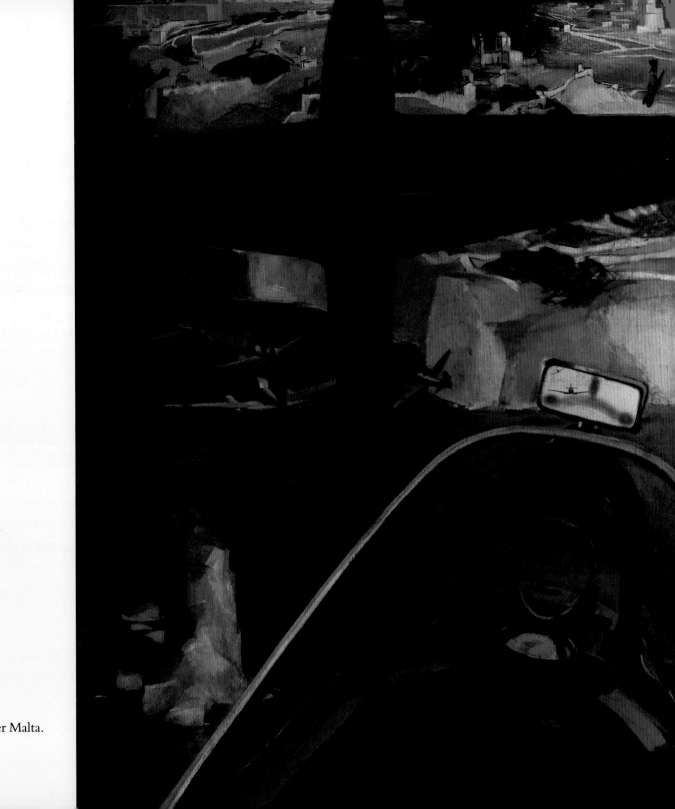

Denis Barnham, Dogfight over Malta.

bravery – until, after nearly eighteen months, Spitfires began to arrive, shuttled in by aircraft carriers and boxed up in merchant ships.

Barnham, himself a Spitfire pilot and a writer, gave an account of the days when the tide in the air war turned. He had trained on Spitfires in Britain and seen action over France, shooting down at least one German plane. But then his squadron was ordered to embark for Malta. This involved getting a dozen of their Spitfires by road and lighter aboard the US Navy carrier *Wasp* and, with a Royal Navy escort, sailing through the Bay of Biscay, sneaking by night through the straits of Gibraltar and then making for Malta. There were still four hours' flying time to the island when the ships needed to turn back, but the Spitfires had to go. None of them had ever taken off from the deck of an aircraft carrier before. As Barnham described it:

Mechanics grab my wings. I am pulled backwards towards the lift. Last glimpse of the hangar, as the floor heaves beneath me, propellers turning, people running, a red sack has been thrown onto the floor down there. My God. Someone must have walked into a turning propeller. I'm on the deck in white daylight. Clouds. Sea. Flight deck in front. A white-sweatered American mechanic, wearing goggles and a red skull cap. He's bending forward like a rugger player, clutching his hands high in the air. His hands begin to rotate. I open the throttle. A chequered flag falls. Throttle wide open, gathering speed, tail up. Grab the stick. End of the deck. Out over the sea. Waves nearer. Stick farther back. At last she begins to fly.

Once they were safely airborne, the four-hour trip was not without incident. They wandered off course and saw beneath them what they thought was part of Sicily, before the twin islands of Malta and little Gozo appeared, and a landing strip. The new pilots were instantly introduced to the reality of war in Malta, for there were three Italian or German bombing raids in the first twenty-four hours which succeeded in taking out three of the Spitfires they had just flown in. Barnham and the Spitfires were almost instantly thrown into the fray. He wrote:

The Messerschmitt 109s seem to have complete mastery in our sky. They seem to fly in a great staircase or net, designed to catch us. First, quite low down, a pair or four, just behind them another pair a little higher, and so on up to 30,000 feet. Mix it with 109s at low level and they can call twenty or thirty of their friends to outnumber you within a few seconds. We can never be on top of them, because we are only sent off at the last moment to attack the bombers.

Barnham was an obsessive painter. He records going out to paint a picture of Valletta harbour:

The sun shone brilliantly and all was peace. Then the sirens sounded, 109s sprinting across the sky. Timidly I was wondering if I should retreat, but the artist inside me said no. Bombs crashed down on my right, and then another stick of bombs behind me made me blot my painting in the wrong place.

His dogfight painting records one of the daily, even twice or thrice daily encounters he had while leading his squadron:

> From 3–4,000 feet I steer the squadron in a shallow dive to one side of the approaching enemy. I can see five big bombers. I can see their fighter escort, forty Italian fighters, but in such a stupid formation – a long diagonal line.

Barnham tried a new manoeuvre which deceived the Italian fighter aircraft. But the bombers escaped unscathed. He later wrote:

> Some inner daemon forces me to go on painting despite the war. I have to put up with the disappointments and utter misery of pictures continually going wrong, as an act of faith that one day I might acquire such skill and experience as will enable them to go right.

Parachutes and Gliders

The efficiency of parachutes increased throughout the Great War and thereafter. The invention of the ripcord allowed a pilot to wait until he was clear of his falling plane before deploying the chute; reserve parachutes were supplied for use if the main one failed; and further modifications allowed the user some control over where he landed.

But these were all refinements to the parachute as a life-saving implement. It was to be a decade after the Armistice before the military of any country started to regard the parachute as a weapon of war. The Italians under Mussolini were the first to form and train a group of soldiers to drop from planes on to a military objective, tasked with capturing enemy strongholds well beyond any existing line of ground troops. The Germans soon followed suit. But it was not until a year into the Second World War that the British, at the prompting of Winston Churchill, formed a parachute regiment.

Albert Richards' splendidly crowded painting of a parachute drop at Brize Norton in Oxfordshire, with the planes climbing away in the distance, was the product of direct experience. Richards, a Liverpool man, had been conscripted into the army in 1940 and had served with the Royal Engineers, while painting a number of pictures on the home front which were acquired by the War Artists Committee. In 1943 he volunteered to become a paratrooper and found himself being trained with the men who were to take part in the forefront of the D-Day landings. The Drop was painted after one of the mass practice days. Richards actually parachuted into France on D-Day itself with the 6th Airborne Division and was involved in the intense fighting around Merville and the capture of the German defenders of Le Plein village.

Richards also painted the crashed gliders which had carried huge amounts of equipment and troops over the beachheads to land in the Normandy fields. The New Zealand Typhoon pilot Desmond Scott described encountering the gliders on the afternoon of D-Day:

> A stream of tugs and gliders reached out from Selsey Bill as far as the eye could see. Hundreds of four-engine bombers were strung in a narrow stream, each pulling

Albert Richards, Crashed Horsa Glider.

Albert Richards, The Drop.

Leslie Cole, A Glider Pilot at the Controls.

a large Hamilcar glider. I overhauled the leaders of this massive aerial armada as it passed to the west of Le Havre and kept with them as they crossed the enemy coast. When the tugs began releasing their gliders, I became so fascinated by the performance of these powerless wood and canvas monsters that I almost flew straight into a squadron of Spitfires. One glider was shot down by flak, but the rest ploughed down into the fields alongside the Orne like a flock of exhausted black swans. Some skimmed along the ground and finished up in a cloud of yellow dust. Others hit the ground at too steep an angle and burst open like paper bags. As the fields became congested, some gliders seemed to have no place to go. But they just dropped down into the smallest of spaces and elbowed their way in among the dust splinters and torn fabric. I was surprised how quickly the tanks left their winged carriers. No sooner had one touched down than out crawled a tank like a crustacean hurriedly vacating its shell.

The Second World War was the brief heyday of the military glider. The Germans developed gliders at a time when the Versailles Treaty had forbidden them to have military aircraft, and in May 1940 Hitler authorized their use in a spectacular exploit which he proudly displayed to the press and the outside world. This was in the assault on the Eben Emael fortress near the Albert Canal in Belgium. Ten gliders, towed by Junkers 52s and each carrying ten soldiers, actually landed on the grass roof of the fortress, and within twenty minutes it had been captured. Various foreign officials were then given a tour of the site. But this bout of vainglory was to galvanize the British and the Americans into a frantic glider-building programme, which was to prove its worth only four years later in Normandy.

Albert Richards survived all the encounters that his regiment endured in Normandy and still went on painting. But in 1945 he was killed when his jeep went over a land mine in Belgium.

The Falaise Gap

Frank Wootton had himself walked through the devastation that he portrays in his picture of Typhoons in the Falaise pocket.

From D-Day the RAF had teams in Normandy looking for airstrips from which Allied planes could operate. Wootton, who had been already involved with the RAF for four years, was able, as an official artist, to get himself to France while severe fighting was still going on. He later recalled:

I went down to the battlefield with the pilots. The ground was littered with burnt-out vehicles and armour, some caught nose to tail in deeply cut roads. The grey-clad bodies of German soldiers were everywhere, some still in their vehicles sprawled over the seats. In the neighbouring fields lay those who had tried to seek safety off the roads.

The painting he made of the Falaise Gap shows the location from which the encircled German armies chose to try and

Frank Wootton, Typhoons at Falaise Gap.

make their escape. The low-flying, rocket-firing Typhoons were tasked with trying to close the Gap, and their tactic was to attack the vanguard and rearguard of the columns of German Panzers, and so block their route out.

New Zealander Group Captain Desmond Scott gave his account of the Typhoon attack:

No sooner had we crossed the railway to the north-west of Falaise when I caught sight of the object of our mission. The road was crammed with enemy vehicles – tanks, trucks, half tracks, even horse-drawn wagons and ambulances, nose to tail, all pressing forward in a frantic bid to reach cover. As I sped to the head of this mile-long column, hundreds of German troops began spilling out into the road to sprint for the open fields and hedgerows. I zoomed up sharply over a ploughed field where twenty or thirty Germans in close array were running hard for a clump of trees. They were promptly scythed down in spurts of dust by a lone American Mustang which appeared from nowhere.

The convoy's lead vehicle was a large half track. In my haste to cripple it and seal off the road, I let fly with all my eight rockets in a single salvo. I missed, but hit the truck that was following. It was thrown into the air along with several bodies, and fell back on its side. Two other trucks piled into it. There was no escape. Our Typhoons were already attacking at the other end of the column, and within seconds the whole stretch of road was bursting and blazing under streams of rocket and cannon fire. Ammunition wagons exploded like multi-coloured volcanoes. A large long-barrelled tank standing in a field just off the road was hit by a rocket and overturned into a ditch. Several teams of horses stampeded and careered wildly across the fields, dragging their broken wagons behind them. Others fell in tangled, kicking heaps, or were caught up in the fences and hedges.

It was an awesome sight: flames, smoke, bursting rockets and showers of coloured tracer – an army trapped in retreat, and without air protection. The once proud ranks of Hitler's Third Reich were being massacred from the Normandy skies.

The Typhoons, armed with their powerful rockets, had come into service scarcely a year earlier. Around 50,000 Germans did manage to break through at Falaise and make their retreat towards the Seine, but only by leaving much of their armour and equipment behind, trapped as it had been by the Typhoons and other Allied aircraft.

More than 11,000 Allied aircraft were involved in the D-Day operation, with 2,000 sorties flown on the first day, 6 June. But the Allied air forces had also been operating across wide areas of northern France in the months before the invasion, not only attacking German transport and supply lines, but also contributing to the successful strategy of deceiving the German commanders – and indeed, Hitler himself – about where the invasion was actually going to take place.

The result, as the German commander Rommel admitted, was that the Allies had almost total air superiority over the battlefield, to the extent that the Axis forces could, by day, only seek whatever cover they could find. Moreover, Coastal

Charles Cundall, A U-boat Surrenders to a Hudson Aircraft.

Command in the Channel had managed to almost completely eliminate the U–boat threat to the invasion fleet.

The Allies were flying Mosquitoes, Spitfires, Hurricanes and the big bombers, the Flying Fortresses, Lancasters and Wellingtons; but also from the landing strips in Normandy came the little Austers, which were the much appreciated identifiers of targets for the artillery on the ground.

But in the days in and around D-Day, there was still a severe toll on the Allies: 2,000 aircraft and more than 15,000 crew were lost before the Germans began their retreat.

Hunt the Tirpitz

Frank Wootton's painting of the Lancaster bombers that finally sank the battleship *Tirpitz* in Tromsø fjord in Norway in November 1944 records the end of an inordinately protracted hunt.

The *Tirpitz* had been lurking in the coastal waters for two years after Norway fell to German occupation, then threatening the crucial Allied convoys taking supplies for the Russians to the port of Archangel.

A pilot in one of the Lancasters was Donald MacIntosh, who described the events of that day in his memoirs. It was the third attempt they had made on the ship. The first time, *Tirpitz* had thrown up a smokescreen, which was totally effective, and the bombers had to return to the base they were using in Russia. A second attempt was thwarted by cloud. But on the third day, wrote MacIntosh:

I turned in for the bombing run, and a minute later, for the first time, I saw our quarry. There, squat, grey

Frank Wootton, Lancasters and *Tirpitz*.

and massive, even at 12 miles out, sat the *Tirpitz*, not a cloud, not a ripple on the water, and no smoke. I saw the long sheets of flame as she fired her main armament. I had to turn away because our aimer wasn't working properly.

Then through the smoke of German flak, they dropped their bomb. MacIntosh's rear gunner shouted, 'She's turning over! What a sight!'

Two bombs had hit her. MacIntosh was never certain that one of them was his, but the greatest threat to the convoys had been finally taken out

Searchlights

Félix Vallotton was part of the group which included Bonnard and Vuillard, known as *Les Nabis*, who devotedly worshipped colour. This picture, which he called Verdun, reflects how, as an official French war artist – although he came from Switzerland – he used their ideas to show the spectacular new technical face of modern war, rather than its grim terrestrial reality.

Searchlights, which had come to have a key role on the battlefield and at sea, were a constant feature of wartime nights. By the outbreak of the Second World War, the searchlight batteries under the control of the Royal Artillery in Britain, and those used to protect many important sites in Germany, had become a vital response to the threat of night bombers. Their beams could reach more than thirty miles.

The testimony of many Allied airmen over Europe confirms how effective searchlights were, not only in holding the aircraft in plain sight for enemy ack-ack gunners, but also in inflicting such dazzle on the attacking pilots as to confuse them about the location of the target.

However, certainly in Britain, there was constant debate about how best to position searchlights. Early experience, during and after the Battle of Britain, convinced some observers that the lights merely helped enemy bomber pilots to see where important targets were. Then a new strategy was developed of clustering lights along predicted lines of enemy approach, and this was used during the year of the great blitzes on northern cities like Hull and Liverpool. But it was always hard to be certain to what extent raids were diminished or deflected by the lights.

War in the Far East

James Morris's painting of the cadaver of a Japanese Zero fighter, consumed in its cave in Formosa, offers a suitably dark end plate to the story of Japanese military aviation – a tale of daring, sacrifice, espionage and theft.

Japan, an ally of the British and French in the First World War, contrived, in its aftermath to seduce the British into revealing the skills and technology of their aircraft industry and, in the cliché of Nipponese industry, not merely copied but improved their machines of war. Then, in a stratagem that was only revealed in 1985, Japan managed to recruit the leader of the British mission, Captain (subsequently Lord) Sempill to act as their spy, agent and source of information on aviation development right through to the end of the Second World War.

Sempill, a Scottish peer and castle owner, seems to have been belatedly rumbled by MI5. But for their own reasons, he was allowed to escape retribution. Indeed, he died in 1965 with no public stain on his character, and it was only twenty years later that public records, finally released, charted his career as a Japanese spy.

Throughout the Second World War, the Japanese had a programme of encouraging artists to depict the exploits of their troops, including the air force. But after the Japanese surrender, the Americans seem to have pursued a policy of collecting and then destroying these emblems of a by then discredited glory.

The attack on Pearl Harbor was the first attempt to knock an enemy out of a war by air power alone – in this case, an undeclared war on an unexpecting enemy. Though the Japanese did use five midget submarines, it was the massive

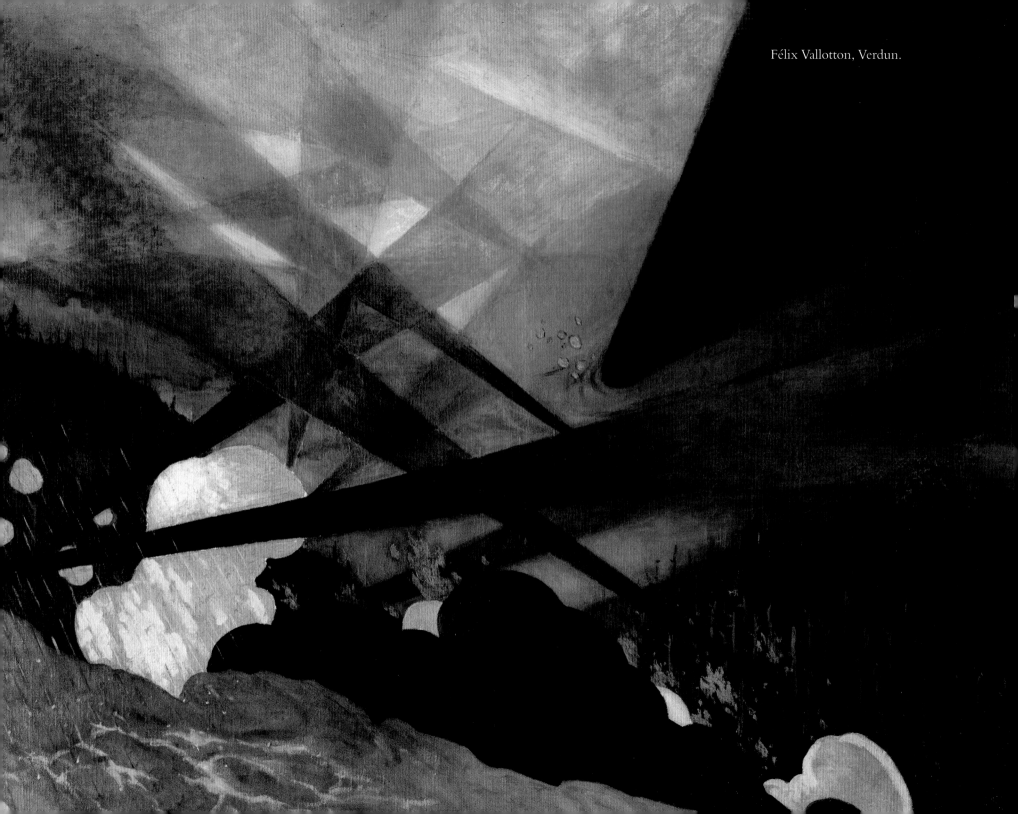

Félix Vallotton, Verdun.

scale of their air assault which was intended to obliterate all possible opposition from the United States in the Pacific. The success of the attack was to all appearances overwhelming. Of the 400 Japanese aircraft dispatched from six aircraft carriers in three waves, all but thirty returned safely. Of the 400 American aircraft stationed on the island, all but fifty were destroyed, and only eight managed to get off the ground at all.

The attacking aircraft also managed to sink or disable all eight battleships and a dozen other major ships moored or docked in Pearl Harbor itself. Information from a Japanese spy on Hawaii had allowed the most precise planning, so that the aircraft came in from different directions to find their targets broadside on and vulnerable, with no chance of offering any serious reaction in the few minutes after the planes came into sight.

There could be no doubt that this was total victory in a battle which came as a complete surprise to the Americans – the 'Day of Infamy', in President Roosevelt's words to his fellow countrymen. And it was achieved entirely by air power, by Kate bombers, B5N torpedo planes, Val dive bombers and Zero fighter aircraft, all launched from aircraft carriers.

But even at the time, as the official American report set out two months later, it was not enough to prevent the recovery of US forces. The docks and facilities at Pearl Harbor had hardly been damaged. Six of the battleships, and many of the other fighting ships, eventually put to sea again. There were no Japanese 'boots on the ground', and despite its further victories, Japan soon found itself on the long road to the annihilation of Hiroshima and Nagasaki. It was to be another sixty years before it could be truly said – in Kosovo – that a campaign was won by air power alone.

The Zero fighter had entered service in 1939 and was used in the ongoing conflict with the Chinese Nationalists. In its first forays it was reported to have destroyed 100 Chinese planes, with only two Zeroes being lost – and those to friendly fire. By the time the atomic bombs were ending the war, the Japanese firms of Mitsubishi and Nakajima had built more than 10,000 Zeroes.

The Val dive bombers, slow and cumbersome in normal flight, and derisively written off by American and Allied experts, were in fact the most lethal of the attacking planes at Pearl Harbor, coming in at 300 feet or less. They went on to play a major part in the battles of Midway and the Coral Sea, before coming to a most dolorous finale as one of the chosen vehicles for kamikaze suicide pilots.

The Kate, too, ended up as a kamikaze plane. But throughout the war it had been the Japanese Navy's main torpedo bomber, and it led the first deadly wave of attacks on the Pearl Harbor battleships, carrying a torpedo with wooden fins, designed to travel through the shallow Harbor waters.

Pearl Harbor represented, of course, at once the announcement and the summit of Japanese air power. But the Emperor's military staff had omitted to ensure that the American Pacific fleet's three large aircraft carriers were also in the Hawaii base. Those three carriers were to prove the ultimate nemesis of the Japanese later in the war in the great battles of Midway and the Coral Sea.

Morris's painting of the defunct Zero portrays the plane which, in its numerous variations, remained almost throughout the war the principal arm of the Japanese aviation effort. The Japanese had a brilliant aircraft designer

James Morris, Japanese Hidden Hangar, Formosa.

Stu Shepherd, Pearl Harbor.

George Plante, Airplane on Carrier Deck, Sourabaya.

in Horikoshi, who came up with new designs which could match or even outperform the US Navy planes which were pursuing the war up through the Pacific islands. He and his fellow engineers produced the so-called Randy and the Ki 83, and even a jet fighter, but dissension and disagreements within the military meant that only a handful were built, and some never saw combat at all.

The Jets

The Gloster Meteor jet was the most remarkable plane to emerge on the Allied side in the Second World War.

It was first flown in combat in the summer of 1944, tasked with bringing down the V1 flying bombs – and almost immediately accounted for at least fourteen, before the V2 rockets appeared to replace them. The Meteor had already achieved record air speeds and rates of climb, and was to go on to display agile performance in the air which attracted attention from air forces all over the globe.

But the development of the jet engine had been a long and winding road for its inventor, Frank Whittle. He had first started to develop his ideas as a young RAF officer in the 1920s, having to explain the concept to an almost universally sceptical audience. But by 1930 Whittle was able to patent his idea, and some elements in the RAF were sufficiently supportive to allow him to go to Cambridge for two years, and also to work at his private company, Power Jets.

By the mid-1930s, the company was able to start building an engine, with companies like Gloster Aircraft starting to think about an air frame, and Rover and eventually Rolls-Royce working on producing a satisfactory engine. But the war was already a year old when the Air Ministry finally contracted to buy a first run of the new plane. It was not until June 1943 that the first Meteor actually flew, and the spring of 1944 had arrived before the first RAF pilots were introduced in great secrecy to the new weapon.

After its successes in destroying V1s, it was some time after the Normandy landings that the Meteor entered combat service against enemy planes in Europe. By this time, the Germans had, more or less independently, developed their own jet, the Messerschmitt 262, which was launched with fearsome success against Allied bombers. In one of their first outings, the 262s brought down thirty-two of a formation of thirty-six Flying Fortresses which were targeting the Rhineland. The 262 was even faster than the Meteor, and in defence of the German homeland in the last year of the war certainly accounted for more than 500 Allied planes.

After the war ended, with the Meteor's merits now widely appreciated by other air forces, Gloster found an eager market for the plane. The Australian Air Force, the new Israeli state and the Egyptians all re-equipped with Meteors. But when the Korean War broke out in 1950, the Australians and the British found that their aircraft were being outclassed by the North Korean MiG jets, flown largely by Russian pilots, which had emerged from the Soviet Union's own aircraft industry. New versions of the Meteor appeared, with new roles in reconnaissance, but it was soon to be overtaken by much faster planes.

Stephen Bone, V2
Rocket Launch.

Frank Wootton, Meteor Jets.

Part III

Post–1945

The Cold War

The Second World War had hardly ended when the victorious Allies, the United States, Britain and the Soviet Union, found themselves drifting into mutual hostility over competing territorial claims and political differences across the globe, from Europe to Africa and the Far East. Hot wars broke out in Korea, Indochina and elsewhere. But the fact that the Cold War remained largely frozen for fifty years owed a great deal to the evolution of immensely advanced reconnaissance aircraft.

The most celebrated of these planes, the U2, remains operational more than sixty years after it first flew. Right up to and beyond the era of satellite cameras, it allowed Britain and the United States to locate and track Soviet missile sites and other key military installations. Able to fly at 70,000 feet, it was for many years invulnerable to challenge by Soviet aircraft, and could cross the entire extent of Soviet territory.

However, the eventual shooting down of a U2 by a Soviet missile in May 1960 produced one of the tensest political confrontations of the entire Cold War. The pilot of the U2, Gary Powers, incredibly survived ejection from his plane, landed uninjured and was quickly captured. Paraded before the world's media, he was put on trial, convicted of espionage and jailed, serving nearly two years before being released in a spy swap in Berlin.

The success of the U2 programme in mapping military facilities in Russia and, indeed, photographing much Russian hardware, allowed Britain and the United States to feel confident that a successful surprise attack on them would be unlikely.

Although advanced fighter aircraft are still, two decades into the twenty-first century, deployed in sensitive areas – the RAF have squadrons in Latvia and Estonia – there have been no outbreaks of aerial fighting between the Great Powers since the Korean War ended more than sixty years ago.

The Falklands War

The Falklands War of 1982 was marked by heroic bravery by the Royal Marines and the Parachute Regiment, including the attack at Goose Green which earned Colonel H. Jones of 2 Para his posthumous VC, and by the devastating attacks with Exocet missiles on the Royal Navy ships *Sheffield*, *Glamorgan* and *Atlantic Conveyor*. These actions were widely

Robert Taylor, Sea Harrier over West Falkland.

reported at the time, for there were war correspondents on a number of ships and with the ground troops. But the extensive air actions which took place necessarily had few eye witnesses other than the pilots and crews themselves. Their subsequent accounts, however, were to inspire some of the most dramatic paintings of the era, especially of the Sea Harriers, which were so loved by their crews for their agility, flexibility and visual impact – even though they were outperformed in many ways by the French Mirage and Mirage Dagger jets which the Argentines were flying.

The Sea Harrier hurtling in over West Falkland in the 1982 war is Robert Taylor's depiction of the Fleet Air Arm plane without which, its aircrew believed, the war could not have been won. Alongside his painting Taylor quotes the account of the pilot, Commander 'Sharkey' Ward:

Without Sea Harriers, the Task Force would have been helpless. I and my wingman, Steve Thomas, were more than fortunate. We were involved in actions which resulted in twelve kills, and we claimed six of these for ourselves. There can be little in life more exciting than a fight to the death, and at no time, when involved in a combat situation, would I have swapped my Sea Harrier for another jet. The jump jet is slower and does not turn as well as some, but it has other attributes which more than make up for this. In combat it will always run the opposition out of fuel and, in a one against one situation, it has an ability to point at an adversary that is unmatched. In a slow speed fight it should always win.

Of course, the aircraft is just a tool. It is a weapons platform which must be used to best effect if it is going to be a success. Prior to the war, I had been lucky enough to be in charge of the operational development of tactics and the training of all Sea Harrier aircrew. My policy had been to concentrate on air combat skills, because this is undoubtedly the most demanding form of flying. It demands 100 per cent effort, concentration and aggression. The pilot must think of a dozen things at once. If he can cope with the combat task, the rest of the operational roles fall easily into place.

Fulfilling these several roles with the Sea Harrier is hardly 'a swan' but it is very rewarding, and I could not ask for a more enjoyable and reliable steed.

The aerial fighting during the Falklands war was of extreme intensity – the fate of the entire expedition was to turn on it. But it was a contest not of dogfights but of missiles. The Royal Navy and Royal Air Force Harriers relied on their Sidewinder missiles to lock on to enemy aircraft; the Argentines, flying principally Mirages, Skyhawks and Super Etendards, were attempting – often successfully – to launch missiles at ships and British forces landed on the islands, but rarely took on British aircraft.

The Argentine planes were often close to their extreme range and were concerned to deliver and then get back home. The British Harriers, keeping an almost constant patrol and operating from aircraft carriers far to the east, were similarly constrained to a matter of twenty minutes or so actually over the areas from where the Argentine planes might attack.

In the crucial days of May 1982, the Argentines lost more than a hundred planes, with more than thirty accounted for by the Harriers; the rest were largely hit by Royal Navy missile systems like Sea Dart, and nine Pucaras were destroyed on the ground by the SAS.

The abiding images of the Falklands War come from the sea and the land – the sinking of the Argentine cruiser *General Belgrano* by a British nuclear submarine, the British cruiser 'shiny' *Sheffield* destroyed by an Exocet, *Sir Galahad*, *Coventry* and *Ardent*, full of British troops and sailors, burning fiercely, their fate recorded by the television cameras and seen within hours on the screens at home. But in the end, it was British air superiority which enabled the ground forces to complete the recapture of the islands. The Argentines ran out of Exocet missiles, and the contest in the sky became a series of duels, with the Argentine Daggers, Pucaras and Skyhawks taking on the British Harriers. Ten Harriers were lost, along with twenty-four Royal Navy and RAF helicopters. On the other side, however, twenty-five Pucaras, nineteen Skyhawks, eleven Daggers and two French-built Mirage jets were destroyed, either in the air or on the ground, along with helicopters and transport aircraft.

In the end there was no Argentine air support for their troops on the ground, as they finally succumbed to the British invading forces.

The Vulcan bomber and its fellow V-bombers, the Victor and the Valiant, were the key to Britain's nuclear weapons armoury for many years in the Cold War's confrontation with the Soviet Union.

The Vulcan's distinctive delta wing shape became a familiar sight above the airfields of Lincolnshire and the east of England as a state of constant readiness was maintained against any threat. But the arrival of the Polaris weapon carried by the Royal Navy's submarines made the V bombers redundant. By 1982 they had been scheduled for the scrap heap.

Yet that year, just months from retirement, they were to be called upon to make the most audacious air attack of modern times, the raid on the Falkland Islands airstrip. While the Task Force was under way, it was determined that a key objective should be attempted first: to disable the Falklands' main airstrip and prevent the Argentines using it for their fast jets. The Vulcans were selected as the only means that Britain had to deliver such a strike. Thus the V-bombers, at the very end of their careers, took on what seemed to many an impossibly ambitious task – to collect 1,000lb bombs from RAF Waddington and deliver them with a fine degree of accuracy on to a defended target 8,000 miles away.

It was plain that, even with a stopover on Ascension Island, the British South Atlantic colony just south of the equator, the attacking planes would have to be refuelled. The only option was to resurrect the defunct capacity of the Victors to act as aerial tankers.

Preparing the Vulcan to carry and deliver the bombs, and turning the Victors back into fuel carriers, meant resorting to every device available, including searching the scrap heaps of northern England, to which key pieces of equipment had

Gary Tymon, Vulcan.

been consigned. It was only after the war that the story of how the raid was achieved slowly emerged.

Fourteen Victor tankers in an elaborately planned operation refuelled the Vulcan and their fellow Victors over the 4,000-mile trip from Ascension, so that the last refuelling before the final Victor turned back allowed a solitary Vulcan to reach the Falklands, execute what turned out be a completely surprise attack and make it safely back to Ascension.

On the way, there had been an unending series of crises, with equipment malfunctioning, several Victors having to turn back, storms which made mid-air refuelling even more hazardous and difficult than it usually was so far from home and, at the last, nerve-shredding fuel shortages in the Vulcan and the lone remaining tanker. But the Vulcan, and its crew and pilot Martin Withers returned to Ascension and then Lincolnshire, to adulatory welcomes from the media. The delta wing became the symbol of what turned out to be a famous victory.

As the fleet approached the Falklands, Commander 'Sharkey' Ward's Sea Harriers had their first clash with the Argentines. As Ward recounted, two of his pilots, Steve Thomas and Paul Barton, were in the air:

Steve called, 'I've got them, Paul. 10º high at 17 miles. 10º right. Judy!' He took control of the intercept from HMS *Glamorgan*. This is what all the months of practice had been for, and now he was in a perfect position to execute the 'hook' manoeuvre. 'Fifteen miles. I'm going head-on. You take it round the back.'

Immediately, Paul took a split to the left, allowing him to build up some lateral separation from the two Mirages, so that he could turn back in on them without flying through their formation. He let his nose drop a fraction to allow the jet to build up more speed, and steadied. And all the time his head was down in the cockpit as he waited for confirmation on his own radar of the target position. 'I have contact! Right 30. Eleven miles.'

Everything was running like clockwork. The only question was whether the Mirages would turn away. Not this time – they were either going to mix it or fly through. Things began to happen fast. The closing rate between the two sets of fighters was more than 1 mile every 3 seconds. Steve had locked his radar-beam on to his prey and at about 4 miles he visually picked out the tiny dot that was the Mirage through his Head-Up Display, neatly framed by the four arms of the radar-acquisition cross.

'Four miles. Visual. Attempting Sidewinder lock.' The Sidewinder wouldn't lock. The Mirage boys must have throttled back, thus reducing the heat coming from their jet pipes to prevent the head-on shot. What about their own head-on missiles? They were radar-guided rather than heat-seekers, and if the Mirage pilot had locked on with radar, Steve could be in trouble.

Just as he was about to fly through the pair of delta-winged jets, slightly low on them, two shapes detached from the Mirages and smoked past Steve's cockpit. Nearly brown pants time!

Then he was through the enemy pair and reversing hard to follow them. He had his control-stick back in his stomach and his head craned over his right shoulder as he juddered round to his right. Meanwhile, Paul had gained visual contact and was turning in hard on the two Mirages from their right. They were not in a good formation; one was ahead of the other and so they couldn't give each other cross-cover. As he turned into them, the trailing man pulled his nose up through the horizon and started a fairly gentle turn to the right. He can't have seen Paul coming, otherwise he would have been manoeuvring like sin – he must have been concentrating on Steve's aircraft position. Very quickly, he was in Paul's sights. The Sidewinder growled its acquisition, he pickled on the firing button and called, 'Fox Two away!'

The missile thundered off the rails like an express train and left a brilliant white smoke trail as it curved up towards the heavens, chasing after the Mirage, which was now making for the stars, very nose-high. Paul was mesmerized as the angry missile closed with its target. As the Sidewinder made intercept, the Argentine jet exploded in a vivid ball of yellow flame. It broke its back as the missile exploded and then disintegrated, before its remains twisted their way down to the cloud and sea below.

'Splash one Mirage!' called the excited SHAR pilot. Then the incredible moment was over and he looked around hurriedly for his leader and the other Mirage. 'Where are you, Steve?'

Steve had turned hard back into the fight, saw Paul on the tail of one Mirage, and then detected the second bogey in a tight spiral descent towards the clouds. This was a well-known and over-used classic defensive manoeuvre. It was supposed to make tracking by a menacing fighter difficult, but it was a mistake.

'I'm going for leader. Below you.'

Steve rolled on his back and pulled hard and down almost to the vertical. He tracked the Mirage and, when his Sidewinder growled, released the missile. 'Fox Two away!'

The little white messenger of death sped earthwards and intercepted the Mirage just as it disappeared into the cloud-tops. Steve couldn't be sure that a kill had been achieved, so he didn't call it.

Ward was now flying himself on the next mission:

'Two Mirages! Head-on to me now, Steve. One mile.'

'Passing between them now!' I was lower than the leader and higher than the Number Two as they flashed past each side of my cockpit. They were only about 50 yards apart and at about 100 feet above the deck. As I passed them I pulled hard to the right, slightly nose-high, expecting them still to try to make it through to their target by going left and resuming their track. I craned my neck over my right shoulder, but they didn't appear. Instead, I could see Steve chasing across the skyline towards the west. My heart suddenly leapt. They are going to stay and fight! Must have turned the other way.

They had turned the other way, but not to fight. They were running for home and hadn't seen Steve at all because their turn placed him squarely in their 6 o'clock. Steve's first missile streaked from under the Sea Harrier's wing. It curved over the tail of the Mirage, leaving its characteristic white smoke trail, and impacted the spine of the jet behind the cockpit. The pilot must have seen it coming because he had already jettisoned the canopy before the missile arrived; when it did, he ejected. The back half of the delta-winged fighter-bomber disappeared in a great gout of flame before the jet exploded.

I checked Steve's tail was clear, but he was far too busy to think of checking my own 6 o'clock. Otherwise he would have seen the third Mirage closing fast on my tail.

Steve was concentrating on tracking the second jet in his sights and he released his second Sidewinder. The missile had a long chase after its target, which was accelerating hard in full burner towards the sanctuary of the west. At missile burn-out the Mirage started to pull up for some clouds. The lethal dot of white continued to track the fighter-bomber, and as the jet entered cloud, I clearly saw the missile proximity-fuse under the wing. It was an amazing spectacle.

Adrenalin running high, I glanced round to check the sky about me. Flashing underneath me and just to my right was the beautiful green and brown camouflage of the third Dagger. I broke right and down towards the aircraft's tail, acquired the jet exhaust with the Sidewinder, and released the missile. It reached its target in very quick time and the Dagger disappeared in a ball of flame. Out of the flame ball exploded the broken pieces of the jet, some of which cartwheeled along the ground before coming to rest, no longer recognizable as parts of an aircraft.

Later, I was to discover that the third Mirage Dagger had entered the fight from the north and found me in his sights. As he turned towards the west and home he had been firing his guns at me in the turn, but had missed. It was the closest shave that I was to experience.

Countering the Argentine Mirages was crucial. HMS *Plymouth* had been sent to West Falkland to shell an army position, when they saw five Mirages coming over the horizon. *Plymouth*'s captain David Pentreath, himself once a Fleet Air Arm pilot, immediately ordered 'full steam ahead' and started to weave his ship as acutely as he could. *Plymouth* shot down two of the Mirages and damaged two more, was still hit by four 1,000lb bombs, but stayed afloat. Pentreath said, 'We returned to the San Carlos anchorage at full speed with thick brown smoke pouring over the deck. Fires raged below deck for more than an hour, with five injured sailors taken off by helicopter.'

Commander Ward described a low level encounter with another formidable Argentine aircraft, the Pucara, over the Falkland Islands themselves:

Steve spotted them first. It was a good sighting against the indistinct colours of the gently undulating terrain. 'Got them, Sharkey! Looks like two Pucaras on the deck. About 15° right of the nose.'

'Not visual. You attack first.' Then, as I spoke, I saw one of the Pucaras. Steve was closing in on the aircraft from its high right, 4 o'clock. I decided to attack the same aircraft from astern as I couldn't see the second target. 'Got one visual now. Same one you are going for. I'll attack from his 6.'

My Numbers Two and Three opened fire in unison against their target, their cannon shells ripping up the ground beyond the Pucara. I had a little more time for tracking and closed in astern of the enemy aircraft, which was hugging the ground and weaving gently – with any more bank its wing tip would have been in the dirt. I had a lot of overtake, centred the Pucara at the end of my hotline gunsight in the HUD, and squeezed the trigger. The aircraft gave its familiar shudder as the 30mm canon shells left the two barrels. They were on target.

The Pucara's right engine burst into flames, and then the shells impacted the left aileron, nearly sawing off the wing tip as they did so. I was very close, and pulled off my target.

Meanwhile, Steve had reversed to the left of the Pucara and was turning in for a second shot from a beam position. I had throttled back, jinked hard right and left, and prepared for a second stern shot. As the ground to the right of the enemy took the full weight of Steve and Alasdair's cannon fire, I dropped half flap. I wanted to get as low as possible behind the Pucara and dropping the flap brought my nose and gun axis down relative to the wing-line. Aiming . . . hotline on . . . firing! The left engine of the Pucara now erupted into flame and part of the rear cockpit canopy shattered. My radio altimeter readout in the HUD told me I was firing from as low as 10 and not higher than 60 feet above the ground.

I pulled off a second time, fully expecting the pilot to have ejected. Must be a very brave bloke in there, because he was still trying to evade the fighters. Steve's section attacked again from the right, but it just wasn't his day – the ground erupted in pain once more. I was amazed that the Pucara was still flying as I started my third and final run. Sight on – and this time you're going down. Pieces of fuselage, wing and canopy were torn from the doomed aircraft. The fuselage caught fire. I ceased firing at the last minute and as I raised my nose off the target, the pilot ejected. The aircraft had ploughed into the soft earth in a gentle skid by the time the pilot's feet hit the ground. He only had one swing in his parachute.

Later, I was to find out that the pilot's name was Major Tomba. He managed to hoof it back to his base at Goose Green after his ejection; before the war was over the man's bravery was to prove useful to both sides.

The destruction at Goose Green airfield was drawn by Linda Kitson, the official British artist. She described the fourteen Argentine Pucara planes thus: 'They lay in pieces from one

Linda Kitson, Argentine Pucaras.

Linda Kitson, Transfer at Sea.

end of the airfield to the other. The whole site was littered with dangerous fragments.'

Kitson was the sole official artist appointed to the South Atlantic war. She had been chosen after doing an acclaimed series of drawings and paintings of people at work, including life at Clare College, Cambridge and in Fleet Street newspaper offices. But she was apprehensive about how she would be able to work with soldiers, later expressing the dilemma she faced:

> I had to make a decision about what aspects of the war I should record. My brief was to record the sights that might be recognized as common experiences. At Goose Green I decided that the horrifying sight of parts of human bodies, a helmet with a head still in it – pictorially sensational and relevant though they were – were not part of my brief. Nor were the war graves. I still question that decision. Would it have been a stronger cautionary record if I had used such shock tactics?

Kitson had come out on the requisitioned liner *QE2*, whose forward superstructure had been cleared away to make a helicopter flight deck. The constant effort to train the helicopter crews, and the Marines who would be lifted by them into battle, became the subject of a series of her drawings. 'The hurricanes created by the rotor blades', she said, 'were a menace, and anything blowing around was a genuine hazard to aircraft. Six hundred men a day would practise mounting and dismounting in full kit.'

At the end of the war she experienced an alarming helicopter trip herself, back from Hill Cove to Stanley:

> I had never been in so battered a helicopter or flown in such high wind with such bad visibility. Captain Drennan maintained a furious flow of invective at the weather and the bucketing craft. As he took it right down to follow the stream courses, the propellers practically touched the banks. I was terrified. And said so. 'There's always a VIP on board!' he shouted back. 'That's me. A Very Important Pilot.'

Kitson was to see plenty of the devastation on the ground in the Falklands. But, by the conventions of the time, she was not permitted on the 'grey funnels' – the Navy ships, including the aircraft carriers.

It was left to the Fleet Air Arm and RAF pilots to try to convey to artists what the war flying experience really was like. The Falklands War was the first major conflict in which the British used helicopters, not only for their crucial role in lifting troops and supplies to difficult areas, and for search and rescue, but also for direct aerial warfare. A British Lynx actually sank an Argentine submarine with a missile strike while it was lying at a dock side. And the helicopters were constantly in action tracking submarines at sea. They were also equipped with over-the-horizon radar, which allowed the naval guns to range with great accuracy on distant targets.

Flight Lieutenant Ian Mortimer was the beneficiary of one of the legendary helicopter search and rescue missions of the

Linda Kitson,
Helicopter on the
deck of the *QE2*.

war. He had been flying a Sea Harrier from the aircraft carrier HMS *Invincible* on a mission to try to contain the Argentine aircraft that were on the ground at Port Stanley airport. But he made one pass too many, and a ground to air missile came up and blew the tail right off his Harrier. Mortimer ejected and found his parachute carrying him some way out to sea. He managed to inflate his dinghy and clamber in, but the emergency radio in the boat turned out to be working only intermittently. *Invincible* picked up the mayday signal, but without any location information. The helicopters from *Invincible* were scrambled and set about scouring the coast and waters off Port Stanley, often uncomfortably close to Argentine ground fire.

Night and the cold of the southern winter were closing in, but still no result. It was midnight when one of the helicopter pilots, Keith Park, back on the deck of *Invincible*, recalled something he had said to Mortimer – 'If ever I've got to come looking for you, Morts, the first place I'll look is off Port Stanley runway.' Park now got himself airborne again, in the pitch dark, more than nine hours since Mortimer had been shot down, and made his way to the waters off Port Stanley.

Down below in the sea, Mortimer heard the chopper. He still had his aircrew strobe light working and switched it on. Almost immediately, the dazzling searchlight of the Sea King helicopter came on, and in a matter of moments the helicopter observer scrambled out, attached the winch to the man in the dinghy and brought him aboard. Frozen but intact, Mortimer was safely returned to the carrier.

It had taken a long time for helicopters, after their first wartime appearance in the Second World War, to evolve into fighting machines. The Korean War saw many helicopters used to lift troops, but they were not heavily armed. By the time of the Vietnam War, helicopters began to appear as gunships, although they were extremely vulnerable to ground fire. In one two-year period alone, the Americans lost more than 4,000 helicopters – more than half of them to enemy ground troops. The Vietcong rapidly identified which part of the fuselage to aim at to achieve maximum effect.

Helicopters armed with missiles proved to be particularly effective at night. In the Gulf War they destroyed large numbers of Iraqi tanks and armoured vehicles, and were a key element in the rapid defeat of Saddam Hussein's army.

Aircraft Carriers

Aircraft carriers were crucial to Britain's ability to fight the aerial war in the Falklands. Indeed, ever since the Pacific war, they had proved crucial in being able to deliver an aerial attack on the most distant targets. From the 'catapult' days of the Great War, when merchant ships were fitted with this device for hurling planes into the air, the value of planes for naval reconnaissance, and then attack and defence, rapidly became clear. But even after all the wars of the twentieth century there was still only a select band of pilots who had ever experienced the reality of aircraft-carrier flying. As the Second World War in Europe was ending, Britain sent aircraft carriers to join the American Pacific Fleet's encounters with the Japanese. One of the British Fleet Air Arm pilots, Alan Swanton aboard HMS *Implacable*, described what it was like to be catapulted:

> From start to finish the launch lasts no more than a second or two and in that short time the aircraft is accelerated from a standstill to flying speed. It is quite unlike anything I have ever experienced. The acceleration is quite smooth but so rapid one feels powerless in the grip of such a giant force. For those few seconds one is scarcely capable of blinking. During my earliest launches I used to think to myself, 'If this lasts much longer, I can't stand it.' Then suddenly it's over and you're briefly imbued with a feeling of complete euphoria.

He was flying the new Avengers. On one take-off he felt the engines were sluggish and tried to abort. But it was too late, and the plane toppled over the bow – the nightmare of all carrier flyers. He recalled:

> As it hit the sea the aircraft righted itself, and quite automatically I started to carry out the drill we had often practised. Releasing my safety harness, I abandoned the cockpit and was groping my way towards the dinghy release panel when the ship's bows sliced through the aircraft like a knife through butter. The water all the way down the ship's sides was naturally very turbulent and I swallowed quite a lot of it as a succession of eddies sucked me downwards. At one point I think I must have encountered the port wing of the plane. I made a grab at it and was dragged back up again.

He then found himself in the wake of the ship, along with his observer and his gunner. All three survived to fight again.

To this day, the aircraft carrier and its planes and pilots remain the principal means for the world's ambitious sea powers to project force and influence worldwide. The Royal Navy has recently commissioned two new carriers, and Ronald Wong's painting of the *Queen Elizabeth* shows her with the Lightning aircraft with which she is being equipped.

These Lightnings, otherwise known as F35Bs, are destined to be the core air armament of an array of countries across the world. They are built in the United States, but with technical and financial contributions from more than a dozen partners, of which the largest is the United Kingdom. The United States alone intends to acquire more than 2,000 of them. The cost of the programme, which began in 2007, has passed $400 billion, with each aircraft costing more than $80 million.

The aspirations for the F35 and its Lightning and other variations encompass every imaginable – and indeed, unimaginable – capacity: air-to-air fighting, air-to-ground attack, nuclear bomber, missile hunter. The plane has the most advanced stealth capacity, to the point of being virtually invisible to current radar and detection systems. By 2019, the Israeli Air Force was already flaunting evidence that their F35s had flown over Teheran, unmolested and undetected by the Iranians. And both the UK and the USA were using them in Syria and Afghanistan.

Ronald Wong, Aircraft Carrier *Queen Elizabeth*.

Their armament can include cruise missiles, guided bombs and laser burners to take out incoming weapons. They can engage in electronic warfare. The British Lightning will carry missiles which can be directed at targets over the horizon, without using the give-away pulses of radar.

The planes in Ronald Wong's picture will be able to land on the *Queen Elizabeth*'s deck without needing arrester wires, by using a combination of their vertical take-off capacity and minimum speed forward air control. The carrier can take a complement of sixty aircraft and is the largest warship ever built by Britain.

The Tornado

The Tornado has inspired its crews and artists in modern times almost as much as the Spitfires, Hurricanes and Messerschmitts of sixty years earlier. This is Keith Woodcock's depiction of the plane.

The pilots of the world's air forces still practise duels and dogfights. They are a central part of the training that the Americans give the airmen of many nationalities at their famous Red Flag airbase in Nevada. Nevertheless, it seems that the era of fighting in the sky – the combat of man and machine swirling and manoeuvring through clouds and the thinnest air – has been destined to last less than a century.

The Tornados of the Royal Air Force were perhaps the last to give their crews the unique experience of eyeball contact with an enemy – at least in practice. John Nichol and John Peters, who were to become, in 1991, the most celebrated Tornado crewmen after they were shot down in the Gulf War

and paraded as Saddam Hussein's captives, had described the sensations of flying the Tornado in lyrical terms; for even in this era of space flight, it is perhaps beyond imagining to know what it is like to sit in the cockpit of a supersonic fighter, let alone fight in it.

John Nichol used to be a star attraction at local air shows telling the fans what it felt like:

It is like nothing else. You snuggle down into your seat and snap shut the canopy. Now you are in a different world, shut off from the outside, with a beautiful cosy electronic whine in the background. In the dawn light you feel the brakes straining to contain 30,000 pounds of raw thrust. Then you are kicked back into your seat. Suddenly at 12,000 feet you break out into that part of the world where the weather is always nice, the sun always shines and the sky is a beautiful deep blue.

But although they had had plenty of practice in fighting, their fate was to be the same as that of all six Tornado planes that the RAF lost in the Gulf War – brought down by ground fire and missiles. John Peters described the last moments of his aircraft after it was hit by a Sam missile while trying to bomb an Iraqi airfield:

'We've been hit! We've been hit!' John Nichol, my navigator, shouted. 'We're on fire!'

The Tornado's wings were still swept back at forty-five degrees. I threw the lever forward. Incredibly it worked, despite the fire and the enormous loss of power, with

Keith Woodcock, Tornado.

the plane lurching back under something like control as the wing surface swept forward now to twenty-five degrees. Then I saw the right engine fire. John Nichol shouted, 'Look out of the side!' I glanced up. There was a bright orange glow in the rear view mirror. The back of the aircraft had disappeared. There was no sign of the Tornado's massive tail plane. Just a huge fireball.

The two men had only moments to make the decision to eject. They were to be listed as 'missing in action' for seven weeks and suffer significant torture, before they were handed back to the Allied forces.

Epilogue

After barely a century, the era of knightly tournaments in the sky, mortal duels in the clouds and the hand of man dealing death and destruction from the heavens seems almost over.

Air Chief Marshal Sir Glenn Torpy watched the Royal Air Force celebrate its 100th anniversary in 2018 with a hundred aircraft flying over Buckingham Palace in London and twenty-two Typhoons making the shape of '100' – 'a fantastic piece of formation flying', he called it.

The Air Marshal, writing the next year about the paintings in the annual Guild of Aviation Artists exhibition, hoped that they could play a role in inspiring people about aviation. Though many of the paintings were nostalgic of battles fought in the sky now half a century or more ago, Torpy thought they still went a long way 'to capturing the mystery and adventure of the third dimension'. He wistfully conceded, however, that from now on 'only a few people will be fortunate enough to regularly enjoy the astonishing sights, the challenges and the thrills of flying aircraft.'

The drones are already being deployed in their squadrons and battalions. As early as 2008, the United States started converting some of its manned fighter plane units to drone operation, with the arrival of the Reaper drone. The Reaper already had true hunter-killer capacity, not only against targets on the ground but also against other aircraft. It also had the ability to monitor earthbound targets, even individuals.

The Russians unveiled their huge Okhotnik drone in 2019 – 20 tons or more, with a range of 5,000 kilometres. The Americans have the Sentinel. By 2019, drones were being used to strike at oil terminals and refineries in Saudi Arabia, and their endurance had been stretched to at least 40 hours or more in the air on individual missions.

The drones not only have no human aircrew, but often no obvious national identity. It is difficult or impossible to be sure which country is actually dispatching and controlling the craft which are attacking you.

The RAF has already decreed that its next fighter aircraft, the Tempest, may be unmanned. It will use artificial intelligence to select its targets, and lasers, microwave and particle beam technology as offensive weapons. The Tempest will be capable of nearly twice the speed of sound. It will climb to 50,000 feet in under two minutes. It will also carry conventional weaponry to destroy the most hardened defences on the ground, to take on anything it might meet in the air and to bomb the cities and workshops of the enemy.

The robot wars are certainly upon us. And the hand of man will direct it all from buried screens far away at home.

Appendix

Cuthbert Orde's portrait of 'Sailor' Malan was one of the few colour works that Orde produced in the course of drawing more than a hundred Pilots of the Battle of Britain.

Orde, himself a pilot in the Great War, was commissioned to draw the portraits as part of an effort to show the British public some of the heroic young men who were defending their skies during the summer days of 1940. He went from station to station, often drawing three or four pilots each day. He wrote admiringly afterwards of the character of these 'ordinary men' who were accomplishing such great tasks.

'Sailor' Malan, a South African Afrikaner who had switched from the Navy to the RAF, was already one of the 'aces' of the war when Orde painted him. He was credited by then with more than forty 'victories' and was to be taken out of the front line to teach new pilots how to win in the air. He wrote down the lessons which he wished to convey in this unique and exemplary document.

NOTES ON TACTICS AND AIR FIGHTING
By Wing Commander A. G. Malan DSO, DFC

Generally speaking, tactics in air fighting are largely a matter of quick action and ordinary common-sense flying. The easiest way to sum it up in a few words is to state that, apart from keeping your eyes wide open and remaining fully alive and awake, it is very largely governed by the compatibilities of your own aircraft in comparison with that flown by your opponent. For example, in the case of the Spitfire versus the ME 109F, the latter has a faster rate of climb. The result is that the Spitfire can afford to 'mix it' when attacking, whereas the ME 109F, although it tends to retain the initiative because it can remain on top, cannot afford to press the attack home for long if the Spitfire goes into a turn. Obviously, there are a lot of factors involved which must govern your action in combat . . . such as the height at which you are flying, the type of operation on which you are engaged, the size of your formation, etc.

There are however, certain golden rules which should always be observed. Some are quite obvious, whereas others require amplification. Here they are:

(1) Wait till you see the 'whites of his eyes' before opening fire. Fire bursts of about one to two seconds and only when your sights are definitely 'on'.
(2) Whilst shooting think of nothing else. Brace the whole body with feet firmly on the rudder pedals having both hands on the stick. Concentrate on your ring sight (note Rule 3).
(3) Always keep a sharp look-out even when manoeuvring for and executing an attack and in particular immediately after breakaway. Many pilots are shot down during these three phases as a result of becoming too absorbed in their attack. Don't watch your 'Flamer' go down except out of the corner of your eye.
(4) If you have the advantage of height you automatically have the initiative.
(5) Always turn and face an attack. If attacked from a superior height wait until your opponent is well committed to his dive and within about 1,500 yards of you. Then turn suddenly toward him.

(6) Make your decisions promptly. It is better to act quickly even if your tactics may not be the best.

(7) Never fly straight and level for more than 30 seconds at any time whilst in the combat area.

(8) When diving to attack always leave a proportion of your formation above to act as top guard.

(9) INITIATIVE: AGGRESSION: AIR DISCIPLINE: TEAMWORK are words that mean something in air fighting.

Get in quickly – punch hard – get out!

FORMATION FLYING. When adopting a type of formation certain points must be borne in mind. The main point is whether you are on defensive operations, or on the offensive over enemy territory. For defensive work, formations should be manoeuvrable and compact. When flying offensive operation the formation should be stepped up and back from the given patrol height and should be divided into attacking and defensive units.

Fighter formations must maintain extreme manoeuvrability, while guarding the dreaded 'blind spot' behind. You'll soon find that if you try to find the answer to the blind spot by simply spreading your machines over a broad front, you'll have lost the first essential, i.e. manoeuvrability. If you choose line astern, which is very manoeuvrable, you'll be blind behind.

At a very early stage of the war I discovered that the only satisfactory answer was to fly in line astern and have the leader change the course of the whole formation at regular intervals.

SQUADRON TACTICS. At this point it would be a good thing to take you on three main types of operation.

First we'll put you in a squadron at 'readiness' on a station in SE England, with bomber raids coming over. If fighters are expected it is always advisable to climb for your height outside the combat area. Your raids are reported at 20,000ft, therefore enemy fighters may be stepped up to at least 25,000ft. If you have no other squadrons supporting you, you should aim to intercept, if possible, from the

Cuthbert Orde, 'Sailor' Malan.

sun – from about 23,000ft, unless you have time to get higher. You intercept and, if there are not fighters present, you must first destroy the bombers' main method of defence, i.e., formation flying. A good manoeuvre would be to attack with a section of four, with the object of breaking up the formation – obviously the most effective method of achieving this is to attack from ahead. But this is generally difficult. The section should go in singly from different angles and attempt to fly through the bomber formation – with plenty of speed, and firing at the same time. With any luck the bombers should break, particularly if one or two of the leading machines get badly hit. The next thing is for the remaining eight machines to work in pairs and attack – two to one bomber. We found that formation attacks did not work in practice, for many reasons which I will not discuss here. Deflection shooting on the whole is a difficult operation, and the most effective form of attack is a diving attack approaching originally from the flank and developing into a curve which brings the attacker, with about 100 miles per hour overtaking speed, 2,000 yards behind and below. At this stage throttle back and, at about 800 yards, come up to the level position and give a short burst to put the rear defence off as you are closing in; at about 250 yards open fire, first at the fuselage and then concentrate on each engine in turn. This was found very effective with eight machine guns – the result with cannon should be quite devastating.

Should the bomber formation have fighter escort, about one third of your formation should be detailed to engage the attention of the fighters without actually going into combat, whilst the remainder go in in two waves, with the same object as before. In the case of the squadron one section of four would maintain height and fly on the flank in such a manner as to menace any enemy fighters who attempt to engage the attackers.

1. Operating from same Station during the raids by bomb-carrying fighters at 23,000ft with escort.

If the Hun approaches from the Dover area it is best to climb well towards the flank in a southerly direction, in three sections of four in line astern on a narrow front, and climbing on a zig-zag course, keeping in a look-out, until a height of 27,000 or 28,000ft has been reached. Having attained your height out of harm's way, the course from now on is shaped according to the raid information. If there is any possibility of intercepting before the enemy reaches his objective every attempt should be made to meet him from the sun and with superior height of 2,000 to 4,000ft. If, on the other hand, it is not possible to meet him on the way in it is best to curl round and attempt to meet him head-on on his way out. It is well to remember that the enemy must come home sometime and usually he has not sufficient petrol to play around. Therefore, it is best to get between him and his home with superior height because, if he dives away, as is usually the case, you can start your half-roll and dive in sufficient time to prevent the fight developing into a long, stern chase. The basic rule applies here as elsewhere, i.e. one section of four will remain up and guard against surprise attacks on the attacking eight.

(NOTE. Had it been possible to gain height in time to await the enemy on his inward journey a good method would be to patrol about two miles up sun from his predicted course in line astern and with the sun on either one beam or the other. A useful hint when patrolling in the rarefied atmosphere at height, and when attempting to search in the direction of the sun, is to raise a wing tip until it covers the sun. It will be found that the area both sides of the wing will be quite free from glare.)

2. An offensive sweep over enemy territory:

When deciding upon a formation for offensive work the aim should be to spread the units loosely, and stepped up and back, or up and to the flanks, having the major proportion on the lower level, and smaller and looser units acting as top guard. Owing to the clean lines and high speed of the modern fighter, an engagement usually develops from an empty sky in a matter of seconds. If the enemy sights and decides to engage, the tendency will be for him to spot your lower and more obvious formations, and miss seeing your light top screen in the heat of the moment.

In most cases the patrol height is decided upon before departure. One of the important points in patrolling the other side is conservation of fuel, so climb and cruise at an economical speed with weak mixture. If the patrol height decided upon were 27,000ft, I would climb the formation to about 31,000, and with the units stepped behind and down until crossing the lines. From then on I would proceed on a very gentle dive to 27,000ft and leave my rear units above and stepped up as arranged, when the lower units would be primarily for attack, whereas the upper screen would always remain up, and act purely as a defensive screen.

Rigid air discipline is essential, and idle chatter on the R/T should be almost a court-martial offence. It is impossible to lay down rigid rules. The two main rules, however, are that each unit must know the role it has to play . . . and that a whole unit should never go down to attack . . . always leave a top guard. If you dive, pull up again after your attack. Don't give away height.

CHARACTERISTICS OF THE HUN. . . . In his training the Hun fighter pilot appears to pay a great deal of attention to tactics. This is a good fault but, unfortunately for Hitler, the German fighter seems to lack initiative and 'guts'. His fighting is very stereotyped, and he is easily bluffed. Another factor is that his fighter aircraft in this war has been less manoeuvrable than ours. There are certain things which it is well to remember when fighting him.

His tactics, as I have stated before, although basically sound, are generally executed without a great deal of imagination, and he repeats the same old tricks with monotonous regularity. There was a saying in the last war: 'Beware the Hun in the sun'. In this war it seems to be truer than ever for three reasons:

(a) The Hun seldom attacks from any direction but from the sun.
(b) The modern machine, with its clean lines and good camouflage, is more difficult than ever to spot against the sun.
(c) With the fast speed achieved by the modern fighter, little warning will be given before he gets within range and, furthermore, it is a well-known fact that the man who knocks you down in aerial combat is usually the one you did not see.

For some reason or other the Hun prefers to resort to what he considers a clever trick to catch the unwary, rather than make full use of his initial advantage and go in with a solid punch. For instance, a common trick is to detach a pair of decoys, who will dive past and in front of a British formation, hoping that someone will be fool enough to follow them, when the rest will immediately do a surprise attack from above. I am sorry to have been caught out by this oft-repeated ruse. I deplore this as a tactical manoeuvre. The obvious, and most effective, action in this case would be for the Hun to make full use of his initial advantage in height and surprise by immediately attacking the formation below him.

FURTHER NOTES

DON'T LOOK NOW! . . . But I think you're being followed.

How many times have we been asked the same question: 'Please sir, what do I do to get a 109 off my tail?' As if we knew. The answer really is: 'Why did you let it get there, anyway?'

ATTACK . . . The essence of dogfighting is always to be the attacker . . . if you find yourself at the receiving end, well, we hardly like to say so, but you weren't really looking hard enough, were you? Or if you and a Hun have met suddenly, your reactions were a bit slow, perhaps. Anyhow, you're up the creek.

Well, we'll try and paddle you out of it. But remember . . . it's quite hard to turn defence into attack . . . so don't start on the defensive. First, when you are practising dogfighting don't continue going round and round in ever-decreasing circles. That's O.K. for a while at least, if you turn hard enough. But you are unlikely to be able to get on the Hun's tail that way, so think up something more clever.

DODGE . . . For example, a 109 dives on you . . . he's got superior speed, so you can't hope to fly away from him. Try foxing him then by closing the throttle and tightening up the turn. He's going too fast to out-turn you, so he over-shoots. Give him a moment to get by you, then . . . stick forward a bit, get behind him and shoot him down. That trick has worked many times.

FACE THE MUSIC . . . Next, if you are about to be attacked, always turn and face your attacker once he is committed to his attack, even if you haven't any ammunition left. Look aggressive . . . that'll immediately cut down his self-confidence by half. As he comes up, turn in behind him. Whether you have any rounds left or not, it'll make him worried. If you have, why, go in and shoot him down. If not (say you're coming back from a sweep), choose a moment when you're pointing the right way, go straight down in a bit of a spiral, pull out, and streak for home. It'll take him probably ten seconds to realise you're no longer on his tail . . . then he has to turn and spot you . . . by which time you're well on your way. If he comes at you again, try the same trick, or pull another out of the hat . . .

FEINT (DON'T FAINT) . . . Such as doing a head-on attack and going down in a vertical spiral directly you pass him. He's fairly sure to lose you. That doesn't mean you don't have to weave though! Keep weaving till you are home . . . and remember, a good look out in time is worth any amount of evasive action.